D1498135

Virginia Woolf

and

Samuel Johnson

Virginia Woolf

and

Samuel Johnson

COMMON READERS

BETH CAROLE ROSENBERG

ST. MARTIN'S PRESS
NEW YORK

First published in the United States of America in 1995

Printed in the United States of America

ISBN 0-312-10741-2

Library of Congress Cataloging-in-Publication Data

Rosenberg, Beth Carole.
   Virginia Woolf and Samuel Johnson : common readers / Beth Carole
Rosenberg.
      p. cm.
   Includes bibliographical references (p.) and index.
   ISBN 0-312-10741-2

   1. Woolf, Virginia, 1882–1941 — Knowledge — Literature. 2. Great
Britain — Civilization — 18th century — Historiography. 3. Stephen,
Leslie, Sir, 1832–1904 — Knowledge — Literature. 4. Johnson, Samuel,
1649–1703 — Influence. 5. Influence (Literary, artistic, etc.)
I. Title.
PR6045.0727Z86715 1995
823'.912 — dc20   94-27520
                                                                  CIP

Interior Design by Digital Type & Design

COPYRIGHT PERMISSIONS

Excerpts from "Patmore's Criticism" in *Books and Portraits* by Virginia Woolf, copyright © 1977 by Harcourt Brace & Company, reprinted by permission of the publisher.

Excerpts from *A Room of One's Own* by Virginia Woolf, copyright © 1929 by Harcourt Brace & Company and renewed 1957 by Leonard Woolf, reprinted by permission of the publisher.

Excerpts from *Three Guineas* by Virginia Woolf, copyright © 1938 by Harcourt Brace & Company and renewed 1966 by Leonard Woolf, reprinted by permission of the publisher.

Excerpts from *To The Lighthouse* by Virginia Woolf, copyright © 1927 by Harcourt Brace & Company and renewed 1954 by Leonard Woolf, reprinted by permission of the publisher.

Excerpts from *The Waves* by Virginia Woolf, copyright © 1931 by Harcourt Brace & Company and renewed 1959 by Leonard Woolf, reprinted by permission of the publisher.

Excerpts from *A Writer's Diary* by Virginia Woolf, copyright © 1954 by Leonard Woolf and renewed 1982 by Harcourt Brace & Company, reprinted by permission of the publisher.

In honor of my mother

Myra Berezin Rosenberg

To the memory of my father

Lawrence Stephen Rosenberg

Contents

ACKNOWLEDGMENTS

◆

This book has itself benefited from many conversations. I would like to thank Perry Meisel, who had confidence in my work from the beginning, and who served as a greatly appreciated critic, mentor, and friend. The Virginia Woolf Society, in particular Mark Hussey and Vara Neverow, recognized my contribution to Woolf scholarship and gave me my first opportunity to share ideas with others who care as I do. Laura Heymann, from St. Martin's Press, was an invaluable editor and reader who motivated me to revise when I was confident that revision was no longer necessary. I would also like to thank Grady T. Turner for his original cover artwork and Frederick L. Brown for his indexing skills. Others have given support that I continue to be grateful for: Joan Kuehl, Judith LaRue, and Enid Stubin.

ABBREVIATIONS

<hr>

AI   *The Anxiety of Influence.* Harold Bloom. New York: Oxford University Press, 1973.

EFP   *Essays on Freethinking and Plainspeaking.* Leslie Stephen. New York and London: G. P. Putnam's Sons, 1908.

EL   *English Literature and Society in the Eighteenth Century.* Leslie Stephen. New York: G. P. Putnam's Sons, 1904.

ET   *History of English Thought in the Eighteenth Century.* Leslie Stephen. 2nd ed. 2 vols. New York: G. P. Putnam's Sons, 1927.

Hours   *Hours in a Library.* Leslie Stephen. 2nd ed. 4 vols. New York: G. P. Putnam's Sons, 1907.

LP   "A Letter to a Young Poet." Virginia Woolf. In *The Moment.* New York: Harcourt, 1947.

LT   "The Leaning Tower." Virginia Woolf. In *The Death of the Moth.* New York: Harcourt, 1942.

Men   *Men, Books, and Mountains.* Leslie Stephen. Edited by S. O. A. Ullman. London: Hogarth Press, 1956.

MM   *A Map of Misreading.* Harold Bloom. New York: Oxford University Press, 1975.

PDP   *Problems in Dostoevsky's Poetics.* Mikhail Bakhtin. Edited by C. Emerson. Minneapolis: University of Minnesota Press, 1984.

Introduction

Though scholarship has placed Virginia Woolf among the greatest twentieth-century novelists, her essays have largely been considered secondary or incidental to the rest of her oeuvre, with the exception of *A Room of One's Own* (1929) and *Three Guineas* (1938), which are primarily recognized as feminist manifestos. Virginia Woolf produced volumes of essays, and only a few Woolf scholars have concentrated on this aspect of her writing.[1] These studies have rescued Woolf from attacks of amateurism and impressionism by placing her within a distinguished literary tradition. But this tradition goes back no further than the second half of the nineteenth century: Woolf is seen as the inheritor of various Victorian values espoused by Pater, Ruskin, Arnold, and, of course, her father, Leslie Stephen.[2]

This study demonstrates that Woolf's critical assumptions are also a product of her reading of the eighteenth century, specifically the critical values articulated by Samuel Johnson and mediated by Leslie Stephen. An analysis of Woolf's essays, diary, and novels illustrates that Woolf is directly influenced by Johnson's theories of writing and speech, that these theories are most explicitly articulated in her early critical work, and that Woolf's early essays are essential to the development of what I term the dialogical style[3] of her most masterful novels. While Johnson is not an exclusive influence on the development of Woolf's dialogical technique, his role in her growth as a writer has been ignored.

The Bloomsbury group as a whole had a strong affinity to the eighteenth century. Woolf's attraction to the neighborhood of Bloomsbury, and the name of the Hogarth Press that she and Leonard ran, testify to her eighteenth-century sensibility. Scholars have acknowledged Woolf's borrowing from Johnson—the title of *The Common Reader* is probably the best example. But Jean Guiguet's attitude, in his *Virginia Woolf and Her Works* (1962), still reflects the state of Woolf scholarship: "Apart from the phrase which she briefly develops at the beginning of her first collection [of essays] and from which she derives the image of the ideal reader to which she repeatedly refers, she does not appear to owe very much to him." Any similarity between Woolf and Johnson, concludes Guiguet, "is a matter for conjecture" (141).

However, there is more than just Woolf's casual reference to the Common Reader. Woolf alludes to Johnson in a number of essays, but it is Leslie Stephen's mediation of Johnson for Woolf that allows for the transmission of particular notions of reading, writing, and speech, the most important of which is the idea of good writing as good conversation. This notion implies a belief in an interaction between the Common Reader and the writing he reads: the writer is in dialogue with his reader. The writer's text is proleptic, anticipating its reception and containing utterances to address that future reading. This writer, as will be argued, is also always a reader who is in dialogue with a precursor, and whose writing is the function of the inevitable pressure felt in that relationship. Woolf's theories of speech and writing are responses to the theories of both her father, Leslie Stephen, and their common literary father, Samuel Johnson. What Woolf found in Johnson's *Rambler, Lives of the English Poets,* and *Rasselas* are notions of dialogue and conversation that helped her creation of a prose technique that places her among the most important writers of this century.

This discussion applies a paradigm of dialogic relations, as it is set out by Mikhail Bakhtin, to the work of Johnson, Stephen, and Woolf, tracing notions of reading, writing, and speaking, and illustrating that these writers are, in fact, in dialogue with each other. The notions of dialogue and conversation will be used to structure what Harold Bloom calls an "antithetical criticism," a criticism that goes beyond source study and the transmission of ideas and images. For Bloom, an antithetical criticism must

> begin by denying both tautology [in which a poem is and means itself] and reduction [in which a poem means something that is not itself a poem], a denial at best delivered by the assertion that the meaning of a poem can only be a poem, but *another poem — a poem not itself.* And not a poem chosen with total arbitrariness, but any central poem by an indubitable precursor, even if the ephebe *never* read the poem. (AI 70)

Bloom's theory of poetry, in which every writer (if "strong") attempts to swerve from his or her precursor to make a literary space, can also be applied to prose. And it is through Johnson's, Stephen's, and Woolf's literary criticism that the initial line of influence is traced.

Though Bloom's theory is often misinterpreted as a psychological criticism, with its premise of an "anxiety of influence," it is not; the "revisionary ratios" are rhetorical figures that operate as though they were psychological defenses. Each rhetorical figure is a linguistic defense used to rewrite, or "misread," the literary precursor. For Bloom, the exchange between writers is based on rhetoric—rhetoric as defense, rhetoric as drive, rhetoric as trope, rhetoric as reading and writing—and the way that each literary text does not function, but *is* a function "grounded in the relationships between a poet, his poem, and the poem's relations to other poems" (de Bolla 22). "Influence" is not found *in* the texts, for influence means "there are *no* texts, but only relationships *between* texts" (Bloom, *MM* 3). This is the kind of influence we find in Stephen and Woolf.

The present study looks at influence as a central concept in understanding the dynamics of literary history. Woolf herself acknowledges that we must define influence.

> Books descend from books as families descend from families. . . .
> They resemble their parents, as human children resemble their
> parents, yet they differ as children differ, and revolt as children
> revolt. (LT 129-30)

The processes of reading and writing are the same. The products—that is, the texts in which the reader and writer interact, are different. The difference emerges from the range of experience the reader and writer bring to their processes, and their interpretations of the world and their texts are always a function of their desire to distinguish themselves, to create a new identity. Though the reader and writer are the same, as parent and child, they are also different. These influences are "infinitely numerous" and "writers are infinitely sensitive" to influence (130). Writing to a young poet Woolf explains, "You have a touch of Chaucer in you, and something of Shakespeare; Dryden, Pope, Tennyson. . . . In short you are an immensely ancient, complex, and continuous character" (*LP* 212).

Influence, as a rhetorical strategy, is a product of reading, and reading is a dialogic relationship between audience and writer. Each component of this relationship has an identity that is itself dialogic—composed of various and diverse voices. The audience, or reader, defines its identity through an interaction with the world that surrounds it, while the writer acquires his or her identity the same way. All identity is the act of placing arbitrary boundaries and limits on the infinite number of influences available. Literary history is the same act of placing boundaries by a narrator who wishes to establish a narrative of meaning and identity. The critic establishes a dialogue between a subject and an audience. The lineage created here, from Johnson to Stephen to Woolf, is a narrative that is as much a function of my experience and dialogue with texts I have read as it is of Woolf's readings of Stephen and Johnson.

The work of Bakhtin has shown that dialogue is "not only direct and *viva voce* verbal communication between two persons, but also all verbal communication, whatever its form" (*PDP* 113). For Bakhtin, "all verbal communication, all verbal interaction takes place in the form of an *exchange of utterances*, that is, in the form of *dialogue*" ("Stylistics" 68). Bakhtin's theory of dialogics is based on enunciation, the context of which depends on three factors: a relation to a speaker, to an object, and the entrance into a dialogue with previously produced utterances (Todorov 51). Johnson, Stephen, and Woolf share common objects, i.e., the activities of reading, writing, and speaking. The objects they share become shifted and transformed, though the enunciation of each is still embedded in the language of the author who follows.

The decisive common trope that the texts of Johnson, Stephen, and Woolf share is that of conversation, or dialogue. This figure is often used as a metaphor for writing, but it is also used metonymically to discuss the creation of knowledge. And, finally, in Woolf, it is hyperbolic, manifesting itself in a literary style termed "dialogic."

The structure of this book is also effected by the notions of dialogue and influence. Influence, as I use the term, is not analogous to chronology for it is not the mere transmission of ideas from one writer to another. As stated, influence has to do with reading strategy and interpretation. For this reason, I begin this study with a discussion of Leslie Stephen's relationship to Samuel Johnson. Stephen's reading of Johnson is similar to contemporary and traditional views of Johnson as we read him in the late twentieth century. This serves as a basis for giving an alternative reading of Johnson, as I do in chapter two, in order to illustrate Woolf's antithetical reading. I revert to chronology—though it is not necessary—when I discuss Woolf's novels. This is because I believe that Woolf's struggle with narrative form is something she dealt with throughout her life, and that chronology clearly traces the direction of that struggle. I do not mean to imply that the narrative found in *Between the Acts*, for example, is a more mature narrative than that found in *Mrs. Dalloway*. The preoccupation with form, between fiction and fact, the creative and critical, was approached by Woolf through a dialogic configuration that she borrowed from Samuel Johnson. The various narrative forms with which she experimented are merely different from each other and in dialogue with each other, rather than more or less developed.

In contrast to Woolf's dialogic reading of Johnson, Stephen's reading is essentially monologic. By monologic, I refer to a reading that strives to unify the disparate and contradictory qualities of Johnson's writing by concentrating on its moral, didactic, and theological aspects. We find his monologic reading strategy reflected in his *History of English Thought in the Eighteenth Century*. There he attempts to understand the philosophical history of the period by setting up a bifurcated tradition that is based on two readings of John Locke. The two lines are those of the skeptical and common sense philosophers. The skeptical school of thought, represented by Hume and his followers, argued that there are no self-evidencing truths independent of experience, and that the mind, or reason, does not exist, but is a socially agreed upon fiction. According to the skeptics, there is no particular nor transcendent order to the world; there is no God, only pure chance. The common sense philosophers on the other hand, recognized that when reason was applied, the existence of God and truth could not be proven. However, they chose not to ask about first causes, and claimed that the "common sense" of each individual would tell him or her what was morally right or wrong. Stephen places Johnson among the common sense philosophers and aligns himself with Johnson because he supports Stephen's strong moral and social sensibility. Stephen argues that Johnson is among those who refuse to look at first causes while at the same time believing there is a moral and ordered nature to the universe.

Stephen is forced into such a reading because of his preoccupation with the theological debate of his own time. He saw the struggle between science and theology in the nineteenth century as analogous to the struggle between reason and dogma in the eighteenth. In his literary and social criticism, we find Stephen applying the criteria of "common sense" to his evaluation of other eighteenth-century writers—such as Defoe, Fielding, and Pope—and in his analysis of the critic's role in society. The criteria of the common sense philosopher are those of morality, education, and social responsibility. Literature, and the critics who evaluate it, should strive to represent moral action and should teach the difference between good and evil. Stephen, in his agnosticism, and in his rejection of skepticism, finds a highly ordered morality in the world. Though in the common sense tradition he refuses to define that moral order, his criticism is an attempt to propagate it.

Though Stephen identifies with Johnson's common sense philosophy, he ultimately criticizes Johnson for his inability to convey that philosophy in his writing as well as he does in his speech, and therefore Stephen reinforces the view of Johnson as one who is remembered for his character and conversation. Stephen finds Johnson's writing weak, and this is because, according to Stephen, Johnson cannot write as he talks. I argue that

Johnson does in fact write as he talks, through a style based on antithesis and balance, where there is often more than one point of view interacting, or conversing, within the text. Stephen's moral, theological, and monologic perspective is a perspective that seeks to unify differences and ambiguities. Stephen is blind to his own insight into Johnson's real strength—Johnson's conversation and the ability to incorporate his conversational techniques into his written discourse. This insight is one that Woolf understands when she reads Johnson. Because of her need to distinguish her literary identity from her father, she is forced to read Johnson antithetically from Stephen: Woolf reads Johnson as a dialogical writer. The dialogical element of Johnson's writing contrasts with the neoclassical reading that began in the nineteenth century with Stephen and his contemporaries and has predominated in the twentieth century. Johnson is traditionally viewed as a moral and didactic writer whose goal is to uphold the classical values. But in Johnson's writing there is also a preoccupation with dialogue, its necessity in creating knowledge, and its purpose in argument. Woolf reads Johnson differently and thereby changes her literary heritage and Johnson's role within that heritage. The implications of this new heritage for the modernist canon are significant, since figures such as T. S. Eliot have read Johnson through the Victorian inheritance and seen themselves as continuing a moral and ethical tradition.

Woolf reads the dialogical and social element in Johnson though the dialogism found in Johnson's work is not fully realized. Johnson struggles to find a method to incorporate the fluidity of conversation into the rhetoric of his prose. His early essays and the *Dictionary* deal with the relation between spoken and written language on a thematic level. His *Rambler*, *Idler*, and *Adventurer* essays reflect his awareness of the potential of audience and its manipulation through conversation, anticipating Woolf's essay "The Patron and the Crocus" and her focus on audience in *Between the Acts*. For Johnson the "seeds of knowledge may be planted in solitude, but must be cultivated in publick. . . . the artifice of embellishment, and the powers of attraction, can be gained only by general converse" (*The Rambler* V: 129). The writer and the audience, according to Woolf, "are twins indeed, one dying if the other dies, one flourishing if the other flourishes; that the fact of literature depends upon their happy alliance" ("Patron" 210). Both writers see a dialogic relation between the writer and audience. The distinction I am trying to make is not between conversation and dialogue, which I at times use synonymously, but between dialogue and dialectic. It is most important that we notice in Johnson's writing the desire to sustain opposition, to allow different points of view to exist simultaneously without resolution or synthesis. Johnson is a pioneer, an experimenter in a narrative style that will find its fullest expression in the narrative of Virginia Woolf almost two centuries later. I wish to show how he demonstrates, though not always successfully, the way rhetoric can be used to present argument in an open-ended and uncircumscribed way, and how his rhetoric helped Woolf to develop strategies that allowed oppositions to exist simultaneously within her work.

Woolf, able to read this in Johnson, took what she learned to develop her own literary style. Woolf's unique reading of Johnson is one that combines both the notion of conversation and the more familiar notion of the Common Reader. Her concept of the Common Reader is the product of two forces: the first is her father, who saw the Common Reader as an ideal person who reads the world with common sense; the second is Johnson, whom Woolf so famously quotes at the beginning of her collection of essays, *The Common Reader* ("I rejoice to concur with the common reader"). However, Woolf conflates Johnson's notion of the Common Reader with his emphasis on conversation to create a concept that is more than a description of an ideal reading process by an ideal reader. The Common Reader for Woolf becomes a metaphor for a rhetorical technique that, like dialogue, allows for flux, freedom, and the lack of stable meaning. Woolf and Johnson have in common a reader and reading strategy that apply common sense and the necessity for dialogue to clarify meaning.

The technique that the Common Reader comes to represent is pursued in Woolf's representation of subjectivity in *Mrs. Dalloway, To the Lighthouse,* and *A Room of One's Own*. This representation problematizes the narrative "I," which Woolf allows to be split, vacillating within itself from one point of view, one perspective and voice, to another. This notion of subjectivity is dialogic, and it allows us to call into question the stream-of-consciousness technique that Woolf's writing and modern fiction in general are noted for. In her later works, *The Waves, Three Guineas,* and *Between the Acts,* Woolf no longer concentrates on the writer's ability to produce a dialogical rhetoric, but on the audience's role in that rhetoric. We find that, ultimately, for Woolf, there is no difference between reader and writer; they are one and the same, and they both participate in the interactive and interdependent process of creation and interpretation. All writers are readers who are in dialogue with the texts they read, and in the act of writing they respond to their reading. Within literary history, there is a series of readers and writers who read, respond, and rewrite the voices and points of view they incorporate — all writers are united into one.

Many writers, Jane Austen for example, have also contributed to Woolf's dialogical style. My purpose is not to privilege Johnson's relationship to

Woolf, but to isolate it from her many other influences. Writers are readers, and writing is always an act of interpretation. My narrative of Johnson's influence is grounded in, and a product of, this principle—that meaning is a mutual construction between reader and writer. I offer this study of Johnson and Woolf as a means for expanding the network of which she was a part, limiting her neither to a matriarchal tradition or feminist perspective for an open-ended style and alternative literary form, nor to the psychological criteria of a more established modernist literary canon.

Virginia Woolf

and

Samuel Johnson

CHAPTER

♦1♦

Leslie Stephen and Samuel Johnson:
Common Sense and Conversation

W
hat attracts those who approach the criticism of Samuel Johnson,
Leslie Stephen, and Virginia Woolf—at least initially—is what
appears to be a democratic view of literature and reading that
comes under the heading "Common Reader." During a time when
readers other than the white male are being included as vital participants in
literary production, the notion of the humble, less privileged, and less aris-
tocratic reader is quite appealing. And the notion of a Common Reader is
the clearest way for us to create a historical narrative among three writers
who are critical icons in their respective centuries.

But on second glance, this easy articulation runs into problems. Johnson
was a conservative neoclassicist who was very much part of the movement
that saw literature as a means for teaching and maintaining a definite standard of values. Stephen, though radical in his agnosticism, adhered to a
Victorian morality when discussing literature. Woolf certainly did not have
the uneducated or working class reader in mind when she constructed the
sophisticated narratives of *To the Lighthouse, Mrs. Dalloway,* and *The Waves.* It
appears that none of these writers meant to include the average or uncul-
tured reader as part of his or her coterie.

Were these writers being disingenuous? Were they using the figure of the Common Reader out of a democratic impulse? What is necessary is a kind of etymology of the Common Reader that begins with Johnson and is then reread by Stephen and Woolf. It is in the tracing of this etymology that we begin to understand what it is that these three writers share. That is, it is only through understanding the differences in their modes of writing and reading that we can understand their similarities and what it is that attracts us to their writings.

Virginia Woolf and Leslie Stephen share a common text, the work of Samuel Johnson. Stephen's relation to Johnson is determined (or over-determined) by his identification with Johnson as a critic and by his self-constructed identity within Victorian culture—Stephen's reading of Johnson is his reading of himself. From his youth, Stephen had a great admiration for Johnson. As a writer who trained himself through reading those he admired, Stephen developed a complex and ambivalent response to Johnson. Stephen modeled his use of moral and didactic criteria on Johnson's. And as a son who both identifies with his father and struggles to find his own identity, Stephen labors to define himself against Johnson. He does this by recognizing Johnson's skill as a talker and conversationalist while at the same time criticizing him for his inability to incorporate the power of his rhetorical strategies into his written prose. Reciprocally, Woolf's reading of Johnson is determined by her relation to Stephen. Whereas Johnson is Stephen's literary mentor, Stephen is Woolf's. Woolf both identifies with Stephen and desires to distinguish herself from his influence. She too admires Johnson, but because of her relation with Stephen she approaches Johnson with separate reading and writing strategies. Her relation to Johnson is not as bound up with her self-identification as Stephen's is, and therefore, without the intense anxiety to overcome him, Woolf finds rhetorical strategies in Johnson that Stephen was blind to. By finding these reading and writing strategies, and by demonstrating her control of them through incorporation into her own narrative technique, she overcomes the influence of both Leslie Stephen and Samuel Johnson.

There are, therefore, two readings of Johnson: the first is Stephen's, a traditional reading that sees Johnson as the great moralist of the eighteenth century, who is known for his vast knowledge and quirky personality and who is part of the neoclassic tradition; the second reading is Woolf's, and it is a dialogical reading that views meaning as constructed through difference, and views knowledge as the function of conversation between various points of view. Both Stephen and Woolf see Johnson as their literary father, but Stephen cannot overcome his desire to be a stronger reader and writer than Johnson. In order to define the pattern of his own reading strategy he limits his reading of Johnson, and interprets Johnson's antithetical writing style as a weakness instead of as a potential narrative strategy.[1]

Stephen's deep reverence and attachment to Johnson is revealed in his letters, collected by F. W. Maitland. In a letter written to C. E. Norton on December 23, 1877, Stephen discusses his biography of Johnson as it is in progress:

> My chief employment at this time is doing a little book on Sam. Johnson. . . . I am half ashamed of the business in one way, for it seems wicked to pick the plums out of poor old Bozzy, and yet that is all that is to be done; and the plums are very fine ones. I don't fancy I am much like S.J., in any way, and guess that he would hardly have attracted me very much in his life-time; but I don't know any one whom I enjoy so much.

Stephen tells J. R. Lowell that he is going to forward to him a portion of the manuscript he is working on: "You know it all by heart already, as it is cribbed from Bozzy; but I hope that you may like to refresh your memory of the old boy—who I specially love." (April 21, 1878). This passage reveals not only Stephen's affection for Johnson and the amount of pleasure he receives from reading him, but also the impact Boswell had on his reading. Stephen sees his biography as an act of "picking plums" out of Boswell's *Life of Johnson*. Writing, as Stephen defines it here, is the act of rewriting, and this is exactly what Stephen does. Boswell's *Johnson* stresses the personality and conversation of its subject. It is full of conversation and dialogue, taking on a dramatic quality as Boswell re-creates the experience of interacting with the great master. A kind of sibling rivalry is found in Stephen's reading of Boswell, who very much wanted to be identified as the literary son of Johnson. Stephen takes Boswell's emphasis on Johnson's conversation and attempts to explain it in more explicit and definite terms.

The early influence of Johnson in Stephen's reading experience is found in a passage from "The Study of English Literature." To establish his definition of a natural, uncultivated Common Reader, Stephen tells us an anecdote about his own experience reading Johnson:

> I had the good fortune, when a boy, to read what is to me, I will confess, the most purely delightful of all books—I mean Boswell's *Life of Johnson*. I read it from cover to cover, backwards and forwards, over and over, through and through, till I nearly knew it by heart; and I should like nothing better than to read it again tomorrow. (32)

These are rare moments when Stephen reveals his almost obsessive preoccupation with Johnson. And we can see that Johnson's ideas and insights
inculcated Stephen's mind at a very young age. Stephen's definition of the
role and function of criticism, which was to teach readers how to live moral
and ethical lives, was modeled after his reading of Johnson in Boswell. In
Boswell's biography of Johnson, which Stephen knew by heart, he found
articulated the eighteenth-century criteria for judging literature, including
the emphasis on neoclassical values such as unity, morality, and mimesis.

Stephen's tendency to read Johnson as he does is linked to his preoccupation with the eighteenth century and his desire to revive interest in the
writers of that time. To understand Johnson's relationship to Stephen we
must first clarify the intellectual context within which Stephen placed him.
Stephen was one of a number of late Victorians who began to modify the
judgement passed on the eighteenth century by the Romantics; Stephen's
interest is founded on what he saw as an analogous relationship between the
Deist controversy of the eighteenth century and the religious controversy he
faced during his own time. Stephen's particular criteria for his social and literary commentary are found in his discussion of the history of philosophy in
the eighteenth century. Stephen saw similarities between the warfare of science and theology in his own time, and the warfare of reason and dogma in
the other—they were the same battle.[2] His *History of English Thought in the
Eighteenth Century* (1876) was an attempt to clarify the history of John
Locke's thought while at the same time having the opportunity to comment
on the religious issues of his own time. He wanted to show that this controversy had its origins in the philosophical thought a century before and that
certain orthodox dogmas had already been dealt with. The other reason for
Stephen's interest in the eighteenth century was that free thought and rationalism did not take hold of the minds and imaginations of a large number of
Englishmen. He wished to supplant the Christian myth, but he feared the
rational scientific approach to life might not be able to engage the English
in the way that Christianity had.[3]

The philosophical tradition of the eighteenth century, according to
Stephen, was split into the "skeptical" philosophers led by Hume, and the
"common sense" philosophers originating in Reid and his Scottish colleagues and of whom Johnson was one of the greatest spokesmen. The skeptics believed that sense experience gives no certainty about truth, and that
there are no a priori truths within the mind. The order of things is arbitrary,
based on chance, and is not a function of reason nor God. Stephen's agnosticism parallels the common sense philosophers in that both are reactions to
theological speculation, both refuse to ask questions that they know cannot

be answered, and both depend on the moral sense. The title of Stephen's collection of essays on agnosticism, *Essays on Freethinking and Plainspeaking* (1908), reflects the influence of the common sense school. The title implies that what is being advocated is a practical approach to thought and ideas. We can trace Stephen's understanding of Johnson and the common sense philosophers back to his bifurcated reading of John Locke, a reading by which Stephen defines his own critical stance.

In his *History of English Thought in the Eighteenth Century,* Stephen states that we associate with the name Locke "the denial of innate ideas" (*ET* I 35). According to Stephen, Locke's greatest distrust is in theological speculation, and he wishes to "preserve a purified and rational theology so as to limit the futile speculations into the inscrutable and mysterious tenets of theology" (36). The language Stephen uses to describe Locke's intentions reflects his own agenda: Locke wishes to preserve a "purified and rational" theology, and Stephen wishes to preserve the same kind of rational theology through his agnosticism. The role of science and empiricism at the end of the nineteenth century caused Stephen to question theological speculation in the same terms that Locke did during his time. It is not that Stephen is rejecting the notion of first causes, nor even denying the existence of some supreme being or essence beyond this world. He is merely advocating a more rational and therefore purer form of belief than the mystical system of religion.

In Stephen's analysis of Locke, the proof of God is the "proof of causation" (36). For Locke, "certainty is only desirable . . . from the comparison of ideas in our minds" (38), not from the ineffable truth of the innate idea, nor from the knowledge we gain from a sense-given experience. Thus, according to Stephen, we have the beginnings of skepticism, for in Locke's philosophy "sense gives no certainty" (38). Hume follows Locke by giving skepticism its fullest expression. For Hume, "chance, instead of order, must, it would seem, be the ultimate objective fact, as custom, instead of reason, is the ultimate subjective fact" (44). Hume, as a representative of the skeptical philosophers, stresses the arbitrary. As far as objectivity is concerned, "chance" is the most certain thing we can know. Custom—that is, habit— is a pattern of behavior. But the order of that pattern is not based on some transcendent, true, or more objective form, but merely on an arbitrary and subjective motivation. The subjective element implies unreality. All perceptions have a subjective element; therefore, "the supposed reality must be a 'fiction'" (47). Hume sees reality as a fiction that is constructed through subjective interpretation. The order and patterns we use to organize experience are also subjective and arbitrary. There is no objective truth by which to judge the world.

Stephen sees Hume's theory as justified "in so far as it denies the existence in the mind of a certain list of self-evidencing truths independent of experience" (59). Hume has the mind emptied of its "supposed innate ideas and a priori truths" and he "fancies the mind itself is dissolved, and that reason is shown to be 'custom'" (54). However, this skeptical doubt, that the mind and reason do not exist, and that supposed reality is a fiction, is too radical for Stephen, who needs to believe in the existence of some essence that guides moral human action. And it is at this crucial juncture of his thought that Stephen reads Locke and Hume, and ultimately Johnson, to help him to articulate his own position within Victorian society. Though he reads Locke as finding certainty in the "comparison of ideas in our minds," he skips this differential conception of knowledge to pursue Hume's similar denial of innate ideas and the skeptic's overall denial of the existence of a unified and coherent reality. That is, he acknowledges in Locke the notion that knowledge comes from a comparison or dialogue between ideas in the mind. This is a critical concept in understanding Johnson's dialogic reading of Locke. Stephen's point of view, however, is blocked by the pattern or order of understanding he has already set up for himself. The subjective element in Stephen's reading, his desire to justify his own agnosticism, shifts his reading away from the notion of comparison to the skeptic's emphasis on the lack of order and pattern in reality. This is what forces him to turn from the skeptics to the common sense philosophers, whose reading of Locke he finds more congenial.

Though Hume may be Stephen's "rationalist" hero, as Noel Annan tells us, the common sense philosophers are often his companions, for they also reject speculative truth and refuse to engage in skeptical doubt.[4] Stephen justifies his own reading of Locke through his reading of the common sense philosophers whom he sees as refusing to question first causes, though they believe that first causes exist. The common sense writers and philosophers, like the skeptics, had "an aversion, to speculative truth" (59). But they also believed that "moral truths must be preserved at all hazards from the skeptical assault" (61). These are the same moral truths that Stephen wishes to protect. Stephen's reading of Thomas Reid, whose *Inquiry into the Human Mind on the Principles of Common Sense* (1764) counters the arguments put forth by the skeptical philosophers, illustrates this. According to Stephen, Reid was shocked by the "threatened dissolution of every guarantee for truth and order" and, therefore, he "attempted . . . to find some mode of escape" (61). Reid's fear reflects Stephen's own because Stephen also fears the breakdown of truth, order, and morality that science might bring to his society. Reid's purpose is "the justification of the ordinary beliefs of mankind" (62), for ordinary men believe in the reality of the external world, while the skeptics had tried to show that this reality was a fiction.

The common sense school was the "natural escape" of the English mind. Its aim was to obtain a doctrine that would give some kind of meaning and unity to experience, and it was a practical application of thought and idea. This is consistent with Stephen's desire to define his agnosticism. It also echoes the influence of utilitarianism on Stephen's thought—practicality and utility are ways of making distinctions between good and evil. Stephen, like the common sense philosopher, believes that there is some meaning and some truth beyond human action, but both avoid probing the foundations of that truth too profoundly or closely. Both Stephen and the common sense philosopher have simply "resolved to disregard a philosophy which landed them in a mere quagmire of skepticism," and they labor to give their practical and utilitarian replies the air of metaphysics. It is a practical yet more ontological reply than their skeptical colleagues have given to the same question.

Stephen's own common sense philosophy is expressed in his essay, "An Apology for Plainspeaking," and is an attack on dogmatic theologies. The essay is written as a response to thinkers who ask, "Why attack a system of beliefs which is crumbling away quite fast enough without your help?" (*EFP* 369-70). Stephen answers by stating that he has "no desire to attack wantonly any sincere beliefs in minds unprepared for the reception of more complete truths" (370). The "truths" that Stephen reveals in this essay are merely truths of common sense, rooted in our experience of this world, not in a world to come. The language of Stephen's common sense is the language of science. The contrast between theology and science is obvious: theology is metaphysical, and "bids us repent, and waste our lives in vain regrets for the past," while science is pragmatic and practical, telling us that "what is gone is gone, and that the best wisdom of life is the acceptance of accomplished facts" (387).

Stephen also desires to rid people of the prejudice that those who do not believe in the dogma of religion are immoral, since "unbelief is connected with bad qualities of head and heart" (371). Stephen is preparing us for his secular morality, a value system by which to guide human action. Equally as faulty is the skeptics' stance that "in these matters a system of pious frauds is creditable or safe" (371). In other words, Stephen does not see morality as inextricably bound with a belief in God. This is not because he sees theology as a fiction that helps people to prepare for a life in another world, but because morality is based in human will and action. What motivates one to make moral and ethical choices is, for Stephen, based on the fact that humans are essentially good. He does not see morality existing outside or beyond the individual, and he does not further question where man's goodness comes from. He knows only that his common sense, what he sees and experiences, shows him goodness, and that good acts are done because of the common sense of others. If Stephen thought as the skeptics do, that all we have are our fictions and that a theological fiction is as good or "safe" as any other, then he would have no faith in moral truth, and it is this faith that he clings to.

Stephen is not a skeptic: though the God and the world of which theology preaches do not exist, there is something else. What occurs when theological belief falls away is not

> an abandonment of beliefs seriously held and firmly implanted in the mind, but a gradual recognition of the truth that you never really held them. The old husk drops off because it has long been withered, and you discover that beneath is a sound and vigorous growth of genuine conviction. (375)

Beneath the skin or covering of religious belief is a conviction on how to live one's life. This is very similar to the definition he gives to the common sense doctrine. Just as Reid attempted to justify the ordinary beliefs of mankind, and to give a purely practical reply to the questions about being and existence, so too does Stephen want to give meaning to what occurs in the world and to state it in a language that is direct and to the point.

A last characteristic that Stephen and the common sense philosophers share is that of the moral sense. Both the skeptical and common sense philosophers saw "the impossibility of constructing a moral code from an ontological base" (*ET* II 15). The common sense philosophers held that vital principles might be maintained, though they could never be proven through reason. The faculty in which these principles resided was known as the "moral sense or conscience" (15). The "moral sense or conscience" is the locus of truth, and so this faculty becomes crucial to Stephen's worldview; it is the moral sense that brings unity and meaning to the whole. This is the alternative that Stephen and the common sense philosophers find to religious belief and skeptical doubt; though reason cannot prove that God exists, there is the moral conscience to guide human action.

Stephen's emphasis on a moral sense based on worldly experience is opposed to a theological morality that stresses the concern for a future life.

> Much of our popular religion seems to be expressly directed to deaden our sympathies with our fellow-men by encouraging an

> indolent optimism; our thoughts of the other world are used in
> many forms as an opiate to drug our minds with indifference to the
> evils of this; and the last word of half our preachers is, dream
> rather than work. (372)

This is Stephen's agnostic belief. Christianity stresses a happiness in after-
life instead of concentrating on the evils of this world. Religion does not ask
people to take action in this world to change what is difficult and wrong, but
rather asks them to sit complacently dreaming of good things after death.
Stephen asks that we don't look for first causes, that we concentrate on what
we do know. Our morality should be used to rid the present world of its
evils, so that we take responsibility for ourselves and those around us. In
many ways, theological belief is corrupt because it produces "indifference"
and causes one to ignore what exists in the world. Theological belief is
decaying, not because Stephen is speaking plainly against it, but because it
is not true. Stephen's is a moral sense common to all and which guides our
actions. Stephen's plainspeaking and freethinking decline to name the suffering of man a punishment for his sins. Instead, Stephen holds that men are
so closely connected to each other that an injury or wrong inflicted on one
is inevitably propagated to others. Therefore, if morality is "the science of
minimizing human misery, to say that sin brings suffering, is merely to
express an identical proposition" (393). In other words, the goal of reducing sin and suffering, as the theologians would have it, and the goal of
reducing human misery through the propagation of morality, as Stephen
would have it, are one and the same. Stephen describes his morality, based
on practical and scientific criteria, with a religious and metaphysical analogy, implying the ontological base of his own philosophy.

Stephen's *English Literature and Society in the Eighteenth Century* (1904)
uses plainspeaking and common sense as criteria for evaluating the literature of the period. Stephen states that his "own interest in literature has
always been closely connected with its philosophical and social significance" (2). Literature becomes a treatise on the nature of truth, and this has
implications for society as a whole. It was Locke, according to Stephen, who
laid down the basic structure for the creed of philosophical, as well as religious and political, thought. Locke appealed to the common sense of the
intelligent classes from his own time to Stephen's, and he managed to
express it in an ordinary language used by educated men. This is what
Stephen strives for in his own literary and social criticism.

As Stephen sees it, Locke's theories were fundamental to the shifting role
of the writer. His influence contributed to the adjustment the eighteenth-
century writer had to make to a new audience. This new audience comes to

be understood in Johnson's work, as well as Stephen's and Woolf's, as the Common Reader. The writer, according to Stephen, had to "throw aside all the panoply of scholastic logic, the vast apparatus of professional learning" (50) in order to speak to an audience that not only wants direct language, but has come to distrust the authority who claims to espouse truth. Here we find Locke's emphasis on the Common Reader who is uninterested in the trappings of scholarly learning and who wishes to escape the power of authority in the reading experience. Locke's influence is found not only on the writer, but in the readers who see the writer as one whose role is to address their experience directly.

There are also political implications for the changed role of the writer in the eighteenth century. The change meant toleration, for it assumed that the educated reader could judge for himself. Intellectually, it meant reason would appeal to something common in all men, and for literature it meant a dislike for pedantry and a greater acceptance for literary forms that were congenial and intelligible to the reason of the new emerging audience. Stephen argues that the "composition of the literary organ" believed in the "Religion of nature — the plain demonstrable truths obvious to every intelligent person" (53). Locke was the spokesman for this literary organ and he held that England was the favored nation marked out as the land of liberty, philosophy, common sense, toleration, and intellectual excellence (53). This reading of Locke, which views him as breaking down notions of writing and the writer in the eighteenth century, asking writers to appeal to the common sense and rationalism of readers, is the same reading of Locke that the common sense philosophers held.

Stephen's morality and common sense philosophy are used as criteria for judging specific eighteenth-century writers. In his essay on Defoe, "DeFoe's Novels," Stephen argues that Defoe's strength lies in the "most marvelous power ever known of giving verisimilitude to his fictions" (*Hours* 4). Defoe lacks passion or sentiment, but he has the ability to see the world with common sense; his journalistic background allows him to give the facts, and, ultimately, this talent lets him tell fictions as though they were true, giving him "the most amazing talent for telling lies" (4). The commentary on Defoe reflects Stephen's mimetic conception of language. He distinguishes between fact and fiction, and praises Defoe for being able to write fiction as though the reality it represented were actually true.

This ability to represent fiction as fact, falsehood as truth, is found in his emphasis on Defoe's perception of the world. Defoe had a

> resolution to see things as they are without the gloss which is contracted from strong party sentiment. He was one of those men of

> vigorous common-sense, who like to have everything down plainly
> and distinctly in good unmistakable black and white, and indulge
> a voracious appetite for facts and figures. (17)

Defoe's style is plainspeaking taken to the extreme. There can be no room
for ambiguity or lack of clarity; language must exactly transcribe the reality it is attempting to reflect. And the only reality there is is the one we see,
the one that can be verified by "facts and figures."

Defoe's mimetic sensibility, which Stephen marks as his strength, also
leads to his weakness—the transcription of fact produces an uninteresting
text, where passion and sentiment could add to the representation. Defoe
gives us "at equal length, and with the utmost plainspeaking, the details of
a number of other positions, which are neither interesting nor edifying" (42).
He is "decent or coarse, just as he is dull or amusing, without knowing the
difference" (42). This qualification of Defoe's work signifies Stephen's own
ambivalent view of the proper use of language in art. Even he knows that
a purely mimetic representation is uninteresting and teaches us nothing.

Fielding, like Defoe, also has common sense, and for this reason he is one
of Stephen's favorite authors. Fielding is able to create such characters as
Parson Adams. The Parson "is simple enough to become a laughing-stock
to the brutal, but he never consciously rebels against the dictates of the
plainest common sense." He has "no eye for the romantic side of his creed,
and would be apt to condemn a mystic as simply a fool" (*Hours* 31). The
romantic and mystical side that the Parson lacks parallels the skeptical
view of the world, where there is something to be known beyond the surface of reality. Stephen admires Fielding for his portrayal of this character
without having to inundate his reader with maxims that explain it. There is
a dimensional quality to Fielding's writing, unlike Defoe's, whose common
sense view is limited to mere fact. Fielding's work contains more than just
the transcription of reality, but also a moral element, where a writer's
"morality must be judged by the conceptions embodied in his work, not by
the maxims scattered through it" (33). The highest degree of morality
"depends upon the power with which the essential beauty and ugliness of
virtue and vice are exhibited by an impartial observer" (35). This is the common sense perspective of the world, as it is defined by Stephen, where
morality exists in a place where all men have common access; and this is the
world that Fielding portrays in his novels.

> Common sense in the highest degree—whether we choose to iden-
> tify it or contrast it with genius—is at least one of the most endur-
> ing and valuable qualities in literature as everywhere else; and
> Fielding is one of its best representatives. (42)

One need not be a genius to have common sense, though common sense is the single most "enduring" quality of literature. Common sense entails a moral sense, and this is the characteristic quality of both Fielding's and Stephen's work. Fielding serves as the prime example of the correct use of literature—to teach through a portrayal of the moral and the virtuous. Pope's writing contains the same moral sense, but it is not as balanced as Fielding's. Pope's morality is "in the main the expression of the conclusions reached by supreme good sense" (*Hours* 162). Stephen continues by defining good sense as "one of the excellent qualities to which we are scarcely inclined to do justice at the present day; it is the guide of a time of equilibrium, stirred by no vehement gales of passion" (162). But Pope's "practical morality was defective" (143), for he is a "parasitical writer" (145) and "one of the most consummate liars that ever lived" (141). Stephen, in the end, compares Pope's moral sense to Johnson's and finds that Pope is not "merely a bad reasoner but he wants the deep moral earnestness which gives a profound interest to Johnson" (173).

Sterne is even more severely criticized than Pope for his immorality. Though we love his writing, we cannot love the man. It is Sterne's sentimentalism that contributes to his immorality, because

> Sterne was a man who understood to perfection the art of enjoying his own good feelings as a luxury without humbling himself to translate them into practice. This is the definition of sentimentalism when the word is used in a bad sense. (*Hours* 72)

Sterne lacks the profundity of a powerful satirist. His sentimentalism is important insofar as it voices a "vague discontent with things in general" (90). But the writing never incorporates the elements of common sense and only offends the common sense of readers; for example, in the character of Uncle Toby, who appears so ridiculous to the "piercing eyes of common sense" (91).

Richardson is also criticized for his sentimentalism and, therefore, his immorality. According to Stephen, he was "the first sentimentalist" (*Hours* 80). For Richardson, sentimentalism was "merely a delight in cultivating the emotions without any thought of consequences" (81). In other words, Richardson has no sense of the moral implications of his work in a practical, common sense application. The sentimental—something Johnson also distrusted—is the excess of emotion without thought. It lacks the rationality of common sense and plainspeaking that are both pragmatic and practical approaches to reality.

Stephen shows us how important it is that common sense and morality be understood in terms of one another, and this understanding is found in his discussion of the role of Johnson during the period. His discussion of Johnson reflects the literary criteria with which he approaches other eighteenth-century writers—that is, common sense as moral and didactic—and therefore the reading of his literary father is a function of the theological struggle he defined in *English Thought* and saw during his own time.[5]

In the eighteenth century the "recognized representative of the moralists was the ponderous Samuel Johnson" (*EL* 157). Johnson is a teacher who

> puts on his academical robes to deliver his message to mankind, and is no longer the Wit, echoing the coffee-house talk, but the moralist, who looks indeed at actual life. . . . He preaches morality of his time . . . only tempered by the hardy contempt of cant, sentimentalism, and unreality, and expressing his deeper and stronger nature. (158)

It is in this passage on Johnson's morality that we begin to see Stephen's difficult relationship with his predecessor. Throughout his lifelong commentary on Johnson, Stephen separates Johnson the moralist from Johnson the writer; as much as he reveres the former, he loathes the latter. Stephen's reading of Johnson entails a twofold response: it allows Stephen to justify his theological analysis of the eighteenth century while he justifies his theological position in the nineteenth; it also illustrates Stephen's preoccupation with Johnson as a writer and thinker, for he ignores Johnson's strengths as a writer and concentrates instead on the moral and didactic qualities of his common sense approach to the world.

Stephen's work on Johnson and the eighteenth century concentrates on their philosophical and theological underpinnings. Stephen reads Johnson as a writer who is guided by common sense principles, and, therefore, Stephen reads Johnson as he reads himself. Stephen admires Johnson's moral sense and, as Annan reminds us, "opposed as Stephen was to Johnson's religion, Toryism, method of reasoning, manners and habits, no man so unreservedly won his praise and affection" (313). Stephen sees that Johnson, like the other philosophers, believed that we

> know not what we are, nor whither we are going, nor whence we come; but we can, by the help of common sense, discover a sufficient share of moral maxims for our guidance in life, and we can analyze human passions, and discover what are the moving forces of society, without going back to first principles. (*ET* II 371)

From Stephen's perspective, Johnson is by no means optimistic about life, and denies that "the business of life can be carried on by the help of rose-coloured sentiments. The world is, at best, but a melancholy place, full of gloom, of misery, of wasted purpose, and disappointed hopes" (371). This view of the world is reminiscent of the view Stephen portrays in his "Apology for Plainspeaking." Where Johnson's world is an essentially melancholy and hopeless place, Stephen's is evil and full of human misery. As Stephen tells us, the world "so far as our vision extends, is full of evil. Life is a sore burden to many, and a scene of unmixed happiness to none" (*EFP* 377).

Stephen admires Johnson because, as he sees it, Johnson is a similar kind of moralist—both are writers whose values are grounded in this world. Much of what Stephen has to say about Johnson's philosophy can be applied to his own agnosticism. Johnson is "as good a moralist as a man can be who regards the ultimate foundations of morality as placed beyond the reach of speculation. . . . whilst no man sets a higher value upon truthfulness in all the ordinary affairs of life than Johnson, no man could care less for the foundations of speculative truth" (*EFP* 375).[6] Both Stephen and Johnson concentrate on truth as it exists in this world, and both refuse to think about what can only be speculated on.

Stephen's agnosticism is based on a firm moral standard, where one's purpose is to better the world in this life. He is not calling for a nihilistic view, where nothing can be done to change conditions, but instead a view that sees the world as it is, without illusions to blur our vision and without the temptation to see our fictions as our only alternatives. Like Johnson, he has no faith in speculation, yet has a firm moral grounding in *this* world. This reading of Johnson reflects Stephen's moral and theological view of his literary father. The strength and confidence Stephen exhibits in his analysis of Johnson's morality does not even hint at his criticism of Johnson's writing style.

Stephen's understanding of Johnson is consistent with Johnson's reputation in the nineteenth century: it is during this period that Johnson became famous, not for his critical work, but for his character. Johnson was the "literary dictator" who dominated coffeehouse conversation. The second half of the eighteenth century saw the end of the coffeehouse club, and Johnson's was one of the last. During his time the society was

> still small enough to have in the club a single representative body and one man for dictator. . . . Talk could still be good, because the comparatively small society was constantly meeting, and each prepared to take his part in the game, and not being swept away distractedly into a miscellaneous vortex of all sorts and conditions of humanity. (*EL* 194)

Johnson was known as a talker and conversationalist in a time when conversation was considered an art. Stephen's reading of Johnson is determined by his inability to relate Johnson's writing style, which Stephen found so troublesome, to Johnson's skill in conversation, and therefore Stephen misses reading the dialogical Johnson, who saw both writing and reading as social acts. Though in brief moments Stephen becomes aware of Johnson's attempt to give his writing conversational qualities, Stephen is blind to his own insight about the origin of Johnson's greatness.

Stephen's anxiety about Johnson is found in his distinction between Johnson's talk and writing. It is this distinction that determines the structure of his essay, "Dr. Johnson's Writings" (1904) and the biography *Samuel Johnson* (1900). "Dr. Johnson's Writings" begins by stating that, as a general rule, "the talk of a great man is the reflection of his books" (*Hours* II 148). It sometimes happens that "a man's verbal utterances may differ materially from his written utterances" (148). But Stephen urges us to "detect the essential identity under superficial differences" for the "talking and writing are palpably and almost absurdly similar" (148). The role of the critic is to learn to know "the human being who is partially revealed to us in his spoken or written words" (148). The essay then claims that it will explain for us why Johnson as a writer appears to be a "mere windbag and manufacturer of sesquipedalian verbiage, whilst, as a talker, he appears to be one of the most genuine and deeply feeling of men" (149). The discrepancy is explained partly by the "faults of Johnson's style" (149). In order to appreciate the "strangely cumbrous form of his written speech, we must penetrate more deeply than at first sight seen necessary beneath the outer rind of this literary Behemoth" (150).

Stephen finds the *Rambler* "unreadable," and Johnson's style a "bad habit" he could have controlled had he chosen to. The style is a "work of bad art" (164), cumbersome and pompous, and owing to the fact that he was writing in the wrong century. His critique of Johnson's writing is harsh, condescending, and judgmental, and it is more a reflection of Stephen's insecurity than the truth about Johnson's style.

> And yet when we have once recognized his power, we can see it everywhere indicated in his writings, though by an unfortunate fatality the style or the substance was always so deeply affected by the faults of the time, that the product is never thoroughly sound. . . . A century earlier or later he might have succeeded in expressing himself through his books as well as through his talk. (188)

Caught in a time that did not embrace his literary sensibility, Johnson's writing suffers from contortions and awkwardness. This, according to Stephen, is the greatest tragedy of Johnson's writing.

However, Stephen does notice that the "most prominent peculiarities [of the writing] are the very same which give interest to his spoken utterances" (183). Stephen acknowledges a connection between Johnson's writing and his speech. This awareness on Stephen's part shows that he has chosen to focus his reading of Johnson in a specific direction—on his moral nature—rather than on how the oral and written skills intersect. Stephen's weak reading of Johnson limits Stephen and what he can learn from his mentor. The problems with Johnson's writing for Stephen lie in the nature of written discourse, and it is the inability of the power of speech to be put into writing that he sees as causing the difficulties.

> It is by no means easy to translate his ponderous phrases into simple words without losing some of their meaning. The structure of the sentences is compact, though they are too elaborately balanced and stuffed with superfluous antithesis. . . . His written style, however faulty in other respects, is neither slipshod nor ambiguous, and passes into his conversational style by imperceptible degrees. (185-6)

Stephen is unaware that his criticism contains the key to understanding Johnson's writing. It is, in fact, the "elaborately balanced" sentences "stuffed with superfluous antithesis" that give Johnson's writing its conversational quality. It is the conversational style that passes into the written style, not the reverse. Stephen will not state that Johnson's wit and rhetoric influence his writing style. For Stephen, it is the weakness, the writing, that effects the strength, the conversation. Johnson is in fact working out a way to incorporate the elements of dialogue, speaker, and audience into his written discourse: the balance and antithesis are a means of incorporating more than one voice, or point of view, into the text.

What Stephen neglects to pursue is the connection between Johnson's conversation and his common sense philosophy. Had he done so, as his daughter Virginia Woolf was able to do, he would have realized that the tedious style, which he criticizes Johnson for, is in fact Johnson's attempt to incorporate his conversation into his writing. Johnson sees the construction of knowledge as a function of a process, the interaction and difference, between points of view. It is important to see how Johnson's common sense is reflected in his conversational method.[7] Common sense, if it refuses to speculate on first causes, begins to see knowledge as occurring in the "distinctions" between points of view. What we find are many truths existing at the same time. This kind of conversation, which adopts the premise of another in order to demonstrate the faultiness of the argument, is used to break apart truths, not to show that no truth exists, but to show that many truths exist at the same time. Johnson's writing adopts a certain rhetorical style that allows the knowledge of his discourse to be created through this process of interaction and distinction. This style may be seen as archaic and convoluted, but it is a style that creates tension, allowing opposing views to exist simultaneously.

Stephen did not understand the connection between Johnson's common sense morality and his writing style. In the biography *Samuel Johnson,* Stephen writes that Johnson sees conversation "as a game, as a bout of intellectual sword-play." His talk was "not of the encyclopedic variety . . . but it was full of apposite illustrations and unrivalled in keen argument, rapid flashes of wit and humour, scornful retort and dexterous sophistry" (61). Johnson's conversation contains the same dynamic and interactional qualities as his writing. But where his writing contains "ponderous phrases" and "elaborate" and "superfluous" (185) antithesis, his conversation is full of "apposite illustrations" and "flashes" of wit, humor, retort, and sophistry. In commenting on Johnson's writing, Stephen points to the elements that make his conversation so extraordinary. Stephen gives a descriptive analysis of Johnson's writing style. Johnson's writing has "lost its savour" for the "mannerism is strongly marked, and of course offensive. . . . Johnson's sentences seem to be contorted, as his gigantic limbs used to twitch, by a mechanical spasmodic action" (167). The problem with Johnson's writing is not only the "mere bigness of words that distinguished his style, but a peculiar love of putting the abstract for the concrete, of using awkward inversions, and of balancing his sentences in a monotonous rhythm, which gives the appearance, as it sometimes corresponds to reality, of elaborate logical discriminations" (168). The "apposite illustrations" and "flashes" of retort become "awkward inversions" with a "monotonous rhythm." Stephen is clearly biased against Johnson's writing, and this is because he has invested himself in the interpretation of Johnson as great moralist and teacher.

As in "Dr. Johnson's Writings," Stephen views Johnson's ornate and baroque style as belonging to another time and does not consider the social and interrelational aspects common sense implies. Instead, Stephen focuses on clarity of style and the ability to communicate through direct language. And with this argument, Stephen reads Johnson as looking back in literary history rather than looking forward. According to Stephen, during Johnson's day the prevalence of common sense forced the writer to be clear, concise, and to the point. Johnson could be "roused by the stimulus of argument" and "could talk . . . with almost unrivalled vigour and point" (172). But in his writing he had an affinity to those "old scholars, with their elaborate and ornate language and their deep and solemn tone of sentiment" (173). His style acquired "something of the old elaboration, though the attempt to conform to the canons of a later age renders the structure disagreeably monotonous" (173).

The "inferiority" of Johnson's written utterances to those he spoke is "indicative of his divided life" (173). The divided life Stephen refers to is that of Johnson as writer and as conversationalist. Even when Stephen does recognize the connection between the talk and the writing, it is only the individuality of judgement and clarity of expression that he sees. There are "moments at which his writing takes the terse, vigorous tone of his talk" (173). Johnson the man was often "sunk in reveries, from which he was only roused by a challenge to conversation" (173). Stephen describes Johnson's thought process as occurring in isolation and passivity. In Johnson's writings, "we seem to be listening to the reverie rather than the talk; we are overhearing a soliloquy in his study, not a vigorous discussion over the twentieth cup of tea" (173). Stephen misses the social and vigorous discussion because he associates it with terse language that is direct and to the point. In his writing the "substance corresponds to the style" (173), and therefore, the substance in Johnson's writing suffers because the style is so convoluted and contorted.

The only writing in which we see a "distinct reflection of Johnson's talk" is in the *Lives of the English Poets.* The "excellence of that book is of the same kind as the excellence of his conversation" (186). This is because the judgements are independent, sharp, and forceful. In the book the "strong sense which is everywhere displayed, the massive style, which is yet easier and less cumbrous than his earlier work, and the uprightness and the independence of the judgements, make the book agreeable even when we are most inclined to dissent from its conclusions" (186). It is the "keen remarks upon the life and character" that are "worthy of a vigorous mind, stored with much experience of many classes, and braced by constant exercise in the conversational arena" (189). There are many passages in the *Lives,* "though a little more formal in expression," that "have the forcible touch of the best conversational sallies" (189).

The society that Stephen discusses in *English Literature and Society* is an important aspect of Johnson's conversational skill. Johnson's skill was dependent on its audience.

He had always . . . made it a principle to talk on all occasions as well as he could. He had obtained a mastery over his weapons which made him one of the most accomplished of conversational gladiators. He had one advantage which has pretty well disappeared from modern society, and the disappearance of which has been destructive to excellence of talk. A good talker, even more than a good orator, implies a good audience. (60)

Thus, Stephen illustrates an awareness of the social and dialogical nature of talk, where what is being said is a function of who is being spoken to. The writer's skill is inextricably linked to his audience. The audience is composed of potential respondents or conversationalists. It is the retort of the audience that the speaker or writer anticipates, and the more skilled the audience, the more rigorous and substantial the conversation will be. Stephen never develops this point; and, instead, he dwells on Johnson's ability to speak as one would describe an athlete's ability in a particular sport. It is the aggressive and antagonistic qualities of Johnson's conversation that he concentrates on, not the social and interactional aspects.

We again see Stephen's interest in the audience in his essay, "Johnsoniana," which was written as an introduction to George Birkbeck Hill's *Johnsonian Miscellanies* (1897). Stephen establishes Johnson's singularity by discussing his conversational finesse and its relation to an audience: "But Johnson's talk was superior to his writings, just because it was struck out in the heat of 'wit combats' with a circle which, even if it took the passive part of mere sounding-board, was essential to the effect" (118). It is Johnson's awareness of his audience, and his ability to use his knowledge of it within his spoken rhetoric, that make him such a great talker. Stephen acknowledges that Johnson's talk is a kind of swordplay in which Johnson's offensive moves are dependent on his auditor's defensive retorts. The audience need not take an active role; its passive "sounding-board" function helps Johnson to respond, essentially, to his own statements. Johnson's "divided life" can now be viewed differently. Instead of understanding Johnson as split between writer and speaker, we can see Johnson's potential split within his own point of view. In the audience, outside of himself, Johnson both projects and perceives himself. The audience allows him to debate himself while never achieving ultimate closure on his ideas.

Johnson's sense of audience is constantly stressed in Stephen's work, and Stephen often uses it as an opportunity to lament the lost art of conversation during his own time.

> The good talker, as indeed the good artist of every kind, depends
> upon the tacit co-operation of the social medium. The chorus, as
> Johnson has himself shown very well in one of the Ramblers, is
> quite as essential as the main performer. Nobody talks well in
> London [anymore], because everybody has constantly to meet a
> fresh set of interlocutors, and is as much put out as a musician who
> has to be always learning a new instrument. (186)

What a person has to say is always a function of who is being spoken to. The
better one knows one's audience, the more strategic one's rhetoric can be,
anticipating and addressing responses before they are made. Stephen's
statement includes the assumption that talk is social and dialogic in its orientation. The reason there are no good conversationalists during Stephen's
time is because society is too disparate; society and audience are constantly
shifting, never giving the speaker the opportunity to gauge his auditors.
Stephen believes that the audience in Johnson's time was more unified and
stable than that of his own. This belief in the stability and coherence of the
audience is consistent with Stephen's desire to read Johnson as a moral and
didactic writer, for the sense of coherence is accompanied by the faith in a
transcendent truth. Johnson's audience, as all audiences, was as varied and
unstable as Stephen's. Stephen's reading strategy keeps him from recognizing the dialogic element in Johnson's audience and work as well as his
own. Though Stephen is insightful enough to understand the importance of
audience in rhetoric, he fails to make the connection between Johnson's
written rhetoric and his sense of audience.

Stephen limits himself to a literal understanding of his literary "dictator's"
value as a writer and critic. He reads Johnson with the other commonsense
writers, framing him within a moral and didactic perspective that helps to
unify meaning in both the world and in literary texts. This moral criterion
for judging literature is found throughout Stephen's critical work, allowing
him to establish the value of various writers and to define the Common
Reader—Johnson's Common Reader—as one who reads for the same kind
of unity Stephen desires.

In "The Study of English Literature," Stephen begins to define the
authority of the Common Reader when he explains the value of "critical"
and "vulgar" judgements of books.

> There is an old controversy as to the relative value of the critical
> and vulgar judgement of books. . . . I am content to observe that
> . . . lasting success with either class is enough to prove merit, and
> that, in any case, the fact that the ignorant have sometimes had the

best of it is enough to prove that an ignorant person may have sound judgement. (*Men* 38)

Vulgar readings, according to Stephen, are contrasted to critical, and the difference lies in the training and skill of the critical reader. However, judgement is not the same as skill, and therefore the less critical readers may find lasting success in their final opinions. The ignorant, vulgar, or Common Reader, continues Stephen, has the "advantage of spontaneity—of admiring a thing because it affects him, not because he has been told that he ought to admire it" (38). To the reader Stephen gives this advice: " . . . read what you really like and not what someone tells you that you ought to like; let your reading be part of your lives" (43). It is Stephen's familiar call against orthodoxy, and the way to be free from the dictates of authority is to trust your own experience, and to test that experience in relation to the rest of your world. The reader, the common sense philosopher, and the agnostic, share a trust in their own perceptions, and a belief that their experience has value, not because it is deemed valuable by someone or something else, but because of their individual sense of worth.

Stephen's prescription for how one should read is reminiscent of Johnson's Common Reader. The Common Reader, for Johnson, is one who is "uncorrupted by literary prejudices." It should be stressed that, for Stephen, when Johnson uses the adjective "common" to describe his reader, he does not mean the average or ordinary: Johnson's phrase is full of philosophical connotations, and so the Common Reader, like the common sense philosopher, refuses to ask ultimate questions and to probe beyond his readerly responses to ask himself how he feels and what makes him feel that way. These are questions for the critic or skeptical reader who tries to understand why the Common Reader responds the way he does and what the writer does to encourage that reading. The Common Reader is practical; he trusts his instincts and responses as a gauge for the value of a piece of writing. The critic is not satisfied with that, and he must look beyond his responses for a more substantial explanation.

The issue of value in the critic's words is addressed in Stephen's "Thoughts on Criticism, by a Critic." The problem with readers and writers is that they "confound the enunciation of their own taste with the enunciation of universal and correct principles of taste" (*Men* 218). The critic's verdict on a piece of literature is not the final statement on the value of the work. Stephen warns the critic not to mistake his personal response for the responses of all readers. The task of the great critic is to "anticipate the verdict of posterity" (219). The critic's task is to understand what it is that will allow judgements to continue through history. His purpose is to describe the nature and process of literary history, not to make value judgements on the work, but to anticipate which works, through time, will reveal the moral and ethical aspects of human behavior.

The critic, however, must be aware of the Common Reader within himself. He must know that a criticism is "only an expression of individual feeling" (221). To see the verdict of posterity is a problem that "is to be felt out, not reasoned out, and the feeling is necessarily modified by the 'personal equation,' by that particular modification of the critic's own faculties, which cause him to see things in a light more or less peculiar to himself" (220). The critic's opinion is that of a "cultivated individual." As an individual, his opinion "should not be dogmatic," and as the opinion of a presumably cultivated individual "it should give at least a strong presumption as to that definitive verdict which can only be passed by posterity" (224). This is not to say that all tastes are equally good. To admit that all taste is equal is "to fall into an aesthetic skepticism as erroneous as the philosophical skepticism which should make morality or political principles matters of arbitrary convention" (231), and this is not the point at all. The critic has a moral obligation to keep "vice, vulgarity, or stupidity at bay" (231), and these qualities, according to Stephen, are not arbitrary at all. Though the critic's ability to do this is by no means "genius," the critic "preserve[s] the prestige of genius by revealing to duller minds the difference between good work and its imitation" (231). We see Stephen filling the role of teacher in his own literary criticism as he points out the moral values and faults of various writers. This is very much in line with his reading of Johnson: for Stephen, Johnson's strength was found in his common sense view and in his moral and didactic approach to literature and the world.

We find in Stephen's social and literary criticism a moral and philosophical analysis, an analysis that does not go much beyond what the eighteenth century had taught him. Had Stephen been able to overcome his anxiety about Johnson, he might have better understood the complex relation between conversation and style and would therefore have himself a more complex critical stance. This is an understanding that Virginia Woolf would grapple with and develop in her writing. Woolf may owe her strength to her father's weakness, for it was her desire to overcome both her fathers, Stephen and Johnson, that forced her to read Johnson in a way Stephen never could.

CHAPTER

·2·

Samuel Johnson:
Conversation into Dialogue

Most would argue that Johnson's influence on Stephen is quite clear—Stephen echoes Johnson's moral, didactic, and mimetic attitude toward literature and criticism. Though Stephen is agnostic, he still believes that the writer has a moral and social responsibility to his readers and that the critic's job is to point out the morally appropriate, or inappropriate, in writing.

Before we pursue Johnson's influence on Woolf, we must first establish the two possible readings of Johnson. The first—the traditional—Johnson, I have discussed in the previous chapter. This Johnson sees the world through a singular and unified lens, where there is an ultimate, teleological truth behind all apparent fragments. The second Johnson is one who finds meaning in the dialogue or conversation between opposing interpretations. By dialogue I do not mean *dialectic*—there is no synthesis between the various points of view. The dialogic stresses the interaction itself, the process, and the simultaneity of differences.

What contributes to this dialogic sense in Johnson's scheme is the dominance of conversation, literal conversation, in the writer's life. During the eighteenth century conversation was considered an art, where the speaker, being quite familiar with his audience, anticipated responses and tried to account for them as well as he could. Johnson is famous for his conversation, and this skill has its effect on his writing. This, combined with his reading of Locke, activates a notion of discourse that is found throughout his writing.[1]

Boswell, among others, has contributed to Johnson's reputation as a great conversationalist. His *Life of Johnson* is full of conversations and dialogues that Boswell believes give the best sense of Johnson's quick wit and personality. He also describes Johnson's method of conversation:

> [H]is language was so accurate, and his sentences so neatly constructed, that his conversation might have been all printed without any correction. At the same time, it was easy and natural; the accuracy of it had no appearance of labour, constraint, or stiffness; he seemed more correct than others, by the force of habit, and the customary exercises of his powerful mind. (306)

Boswell's description reminds us how refined and developed Johnson's conversation was. According to Boswell, Johnson's conversation was so thought out and well constructed that it could be printed without revision. Even Boswell sees that Johnson's talk and writing have similarities that reflect the power and structure of his mind.

Boswell also gives us Johnson's own views on conversation. Johnson tells us that in conversation there must first be "knowledge, there must be materials"; second, there must be "a command of words"; third, there should be "imagination, to place things in such views as they are not commonly seen in"; and lastly, there must be "presence of mind, and a resolution that is not to be overcome by failures" (285). For Johnson too there is a difference between talk and conversation, for he would complain of a dinner party that he had "talk enough, but no conversation; there was nothing discussed" (291). This distinction illustrates that the notion of conversation entails exchange and interaction, while mere talk does not. Conversation entails knowledge, imagination, and a command of words. What talk lacks is the element of eighteenth-century wit. Without the substance of content, and the language to communicate it in a convincing and mind-provoking manner, talk remains empty and does not achieve the level of conversation.

Johnson's periodical essays, the *Rambler, Adventurer,* and *Idler,* written between 1750 and 1760, mark the beginning of his ideas on conversation and its relation to writing and reading. Johnson's aptitude and need for conversation are well documented.[2] Johnson was obsessed with fears of insanity and doubts about salvation, and often found solace in the busy, social world of the coffeehouse. Conversation, when Johnson uses the term, is always full of social and colloquial connotations. When Johnson entered into conversation he escaped the passive and isolated world of his obsessions, and his thought process was engaged in a communal activity. The conversationalist can in some ways be paralleled to the man of action and politics. To be successful in either profession, intercourse with other men is necessary and based on the same elements of human nature. For example, the converser, like the politician, may "repress a rival, or obstruct a follower" using "artifices so gross and mean" so as to receive veneration from the world, even though he has not superior intelligence (*The Rambler* III: 117). Like the politician, the person engaged in conversation causes change or action through language. The effect language has on the auditor is based on the speaker's relationship with his listener. What the speaker says, or the politician does, is a function of whom he is speaking to, and his awareness of this determines how successful he will be.

Johnson's personal need for conversation is reflected in his discussion of the man who needs conversation to escape the creations of his imagination. Johnson writes of the development of human behavior: a man "must teach his desires to fix upon external things; he must adopt the joys and pains of others, and excite in his mind the want of social pleasures and amicable communication" (IV: 107). The most "eligible amusement of a rational being seems to be that interchange of thoughts which is practised in free and easy conversation . . . where everyman speaks with no other restraint than unwillingness to offend, and hears no other disposition than desire to be pleased" (IV: 108). For Johnson, the greatest pleasure of the rational and thinking man is to enter into the social world of conversation. In order for the writer and thinker to be complete, he must empathize with the joys and sorrows of other men and create in himself the desire to interact with others.

Therefore, in order for the learned man or writer to be complete, he must converse or interact with other men. A letter from Vivaculus to Mr. Rambler in essay No. 177 states that the author realizes he must have interaction with other men, but that the men he comes into contact with are limited in their knowledge. For Mr. Rambler (i.e., Johnson), the extent of knowledge belonging to a speaker's listener doesn't matter, as long as one is doing the best one can, busying his mind without corrupting it.

The construction of knowledge through conversation is a social act, and it is also based on a dialogic process. In *The Rambler* Johnson repeats the fact that the "seeds of knowledge may be planted in solitude, but must be cultivated in publick. . . . the artifice of embellishment, and the powers of attraction, can be gained only by general converse" (V: 129). The "experience which can never be attained by solitary diligence . . . must arise from general converse, and accurate observation of the living world" (III: 20). The danger is that he "that devotes himself to retired study naturally sinks from omission to forgetfulness of social duties; he must be therefore sometimes awakened, and recalled to the general condition of mankind" (V: 181). Learned men must interact with common men: "He that can only converse upon questions, about which only a small part of mankind has knowledge sufficient to make them curious, must lose his days in unsocial silence, and live in the crowd of life without a companion" (IV: 364). It is at this juncture that the traditional and dialogical Johnson merge—there is still the concern for behavior and how thought manifests itself in the world and how the world manifests itself in thought.

Johnson also sees a connection between conversation and writing: study, composition, and converse are equally necessary to intellectual accomplishment. In *The Adventurer* No. 85, Johnson describes how men of learning discourse "as if they thought every other man had been employed in the same inquiries" (414). His view of the dialogic nature of knowledge begins to emerge when he discusses the isolated man who "comes into the world among men who, arguing upon dissimilar principles, have been led to different conclusions, and being placed in various situations view the same object on many sides . . . [the isolated man] finds his darling position attacked, and himself in no condition to defend it" (415). The isolated man cannot construct for himself the many varied positions he needs to develop a strong argument. When he finds himself among those with a different point of view he doesn't know how to account for them. Here we find Johnson acknowledging that there are multiple points of view on a single subject, not just one truth about it. If there were one truth and one way of looking at things, the solitary thinker would have no problem, for he would be inspired by the single truth that informs all thinkers.

Conversation is essential, for it strengthens argument by producing a foil with which one can reflect one's own point of view. The solitary man is "perplexed and amazed by a new posture of an antagonist" (415). Only by having experience in changing a stated position into various forms, attempting to present different points of view, and connecting it to known truths can the writer develop himself. He who has "collected his knowledge in solitude, must learn its application by mixing with mankind" (416). The dialogic nature of knowledge lies in the fact that ideas emerge only with the interaction of varying points of view.

Conversation is essential not only to the acquisition of knowledge, but also to its creation. Those who participate in conversation must "contribute to its production, since the mind stagnates without external ventilation, and that effervescence of the fancy, which flashes into transport, can be raised only by the infusion of dissimilar ideas" (*The Rambler* IV: 178). Conversation creates what we know because we are constantly interacting with opinions that are dissimilar from our own. The creation of knowledge through conversation is the "lustre of moral and religious truth" that is found in the "interaction with common life" (V: 186). These truths are gained not through solitary meditation, but by a process of mixing with mankind. For Johnson the dialogist and common sense philosopher, truth and morality come through these social interactions rather than, as the skeptical philosophers would have it, through logic and reason. This notion of knowledge as process is developed further as Johnson gains a greater awareness of how meaning is created; it is his experience as a lexicographer that awakens him to the unstable nature of language.

While Johnson was working on his periodical essays, he was also planning and writing his famous *Dictionary*. In 1746 he wrote "A Short Scheme for Compiling a New Dictionary of the English Language" and in 1747 published it as "The Plan of a Dictionary." The *Dictionary* was published in 1755. During this nine-year span, Johnson's view on the nature of language changed radically from a belief that he could "fix" the meaning of a word to the knowledge that meaning is endlessly deferred. His initial view was that of the traditional Johnson, for in a world where there is an ultimate truth, it is crucial that every word have the same meaning for every person who uses it. This kind of communication is what Johnson hoped he would achieve with the completion of the *Dictionary*. That is, with the influx of the French language and lower-class English dialects, many thinkers, including Johnson, feared the deterioration of the English language. Johnson's *Dictionary* was conceived as a means to stabilize and preserve the original meaning of his native tongue; he believed that by bringing purity to the language he could bring us closer to an ideal world.

"The Plan of a Dictionary" explicitly states Johnson's intention as a lexicographer. In order to achieve the kind of communication desired, where language is free from all pedantries and technicalities so as to allow members of diverse social classes to understand one another, a dictionary must be of "advantage to the common workman" (5). It is the unlearned who "much oftener consult their dictionaries, for the meaning of words, than for their structures or formations" (5). Johnson's lifelong concern for the Common Reader is found in his desire to design the *Dictionary* "not merely for critics but for popular use" (7). Therefore, when Johnson wrote the "Plan," he believed that in orthography, etymology, and pronunciation, the "one great end of this undertaking is to fix the English language" (11).[3] After eight years of struggle, he would come to understand the nature of language much more thoroughly and acknowledge the impossibility of fixing its meaning.

The *Dictionary* itself was conceived in an encyclopedic tradition that had "educational aims and identifies students as an important part of [its] audience" (DeMaria 11). That is, it was the Common Reader, not a specialist in any technical field, whom Johnson considered the audience for his dictionary. These educational concerns are consistent with Johnson's overall "life of writing." Johnson "often saw his position as a writer in society as an educational position" (18). Robert DeMaria's lexicographical study catalogues various topics that are part of the *Dictionary*'s pedagogical nature. He identifies the central concerns as "knowledge and ignorance, truth and probability, learning and education, language, religion and morality" (x).

What is most interesting about DeMaria's study is its discussion of the genre of the *Dictionary*. He finds the *Dictionary* containing "a certain degree of self-conscious irony" through which Johnson wishes to "satirize the lexicographer's task" (26). DeMaria argues that such self-conscious irony puts the *Dictionary* in a class of encyclopedic works that Northrop Frye identifies as Menippean satire. The use of satire, as DeMaria explains it, entails another dialogic configuration that allows Johnson to communicate the meanings in his *Dictionary*. It is usually in the form of a dialogue or colloquy, in which the dramatic interest is in a conflict of ideas rather than character. DeMaria believes the short form of the Menippean satire is also found in Johnson's *Irene, Rasselas*, essays, and "The Vanity of Human Wishes," as well as passages in the *Dictionary*, "where successive speakers seem to engage one another in an intellectual colloquy" (27). Like the isolated writer and thinker in Johnson's periodical essays, the voices found in the *Dictionary* must interact with other voices in order to find their structure and form.

Johnson achieves this sense of colloquy and difference through the numerous quotations he places under each word in the *Dictionary*. Each quotation contains a different connotation of the word being defined, and each echoes and resonates meaning in relation to the others. For instance, under the verb *to converse*, Johnson has the following:

1. *To cohabit with; to hold intercourse with.* —Locke
2. *To be acquainted with.* —Shakespeare
3. *To convey thoughts reciprocally in talk.* —Milton
4. *To discourse familiarly upon any subject.* —Dryden
5. *To have commerce with a different sex.* —Guardian

By lining up the various voices in order to define the word *converse*, the context in which each word is used blends and mixes with the others. For example, not only does *converse* mean to talk knowledgeably about a subject, as Dryden defines it, but, according to Milton, it also means the "interchange" of ideas. The definition of *converse* can be expanded if we look at the connotations of Locke's definition, "cohabit" — not only do meanings interact with each other, but they live with and in each other. Finally, the sexual connotations of *converse* in terms of language refer to a mixing and interchange of two formerly separate bodies (words) to create a third, and totally new and separate, entity. The meanings of these quotes actually mimic the very thing they are describing. It is the differences between these connotations that help us to understand the meaning of the word. There is under each definition in the *Dictionary* a juxtaposition of voices through quotations from various authors. Johnson does this to give examples of the various connotative meanings of each word through voices that are not his own. Johnson's *Dictionary* begins to reveal a sophisticated conception of dialogue as a means for communicating meaning. This conception is the result of both his failure to fix the origins of words, which he attempted to do in his eight years before completing the project, and his reading of John Locke.

It is in the *Dictionary* that we see Johnson's awareness that he cannot fix language, and it could be argued that Locke's *Essay Concerning Human Understanding*, particularly Book III, "Of Words," was a major influence on the dialogical mode of thought that came to replace Johnson's earlier conception of language as unified and fixed. There are a number of references to Locke in the dictionary — such as those found under these entries: appellations, affect, advance, confound, certainty, corrupt, correspond, express, exchange, name, nothing, and relate — and DeMaria persuasively argues Locke's influence in the *Dictionary*.[4] Locke's philosophy permeates Johnson's writing, as well as the writing of Johnson's contemporaries.[5]

Locke's theory of knowledge as process allows Johnson to see knowledge as a function of conversation and dialogue, where knowledge is not one point of view or another, but an interaction between points of view. Locke's philosophy begins with a denial of innate ideas, and he substitutes the notion of innate ideas with a theory of knowledge as process. He argues that truth is found in "the joining and separating of signs, as the things signified by them do agree and disagree with one another" (277). Johnson, who by the time he wrote the Preface to the *Dictionary* believed it was impossible to find the original meaning of a word, may have agreed with Locke that "words, in their primary or immediate signification, stand for nothing but *the ideas in the mind of him that uses them*," and are not "marks of the ideas in the minds also of other men" nor "stand for the reality of things" (205). Words do not have the same meanings for different readers; there is no transcendental meaning.

Meaning can be achieved only through the intermixing and juxtaposition of various signs, allowing a dialogue between them to create both harmony and discord, much as the various contexts for the use of the word *converse* show us the meaning of that word.

In Lockean theory, the products of mixed significations or ideas are called "mixed modes," and unlike simple ideas, which are the closest we can get to original meaning, they are "made by understanding" (219), that is, made by the mind. Mixed modes are made for the "convenience of communication" (220) and are "collections made and abstracted by the mind" and not "the steady workmanship of nature" (221). Language, therefore, has no natural or original meaning, but is a social institution created by man in order to communicate with other men.[6] For Johnson and Locke, the "ends of language in our discourse with others [is] . . . to make known one man's thoughts or ideas to another . . . to do it with as much ease and quickness as possible . . . thereby to convey the knowledge of things" (245). Locke's views of knowledge and meaning as process and language as a social and moral institution are found throughout the *Dictionary*.[7]

Johnson's dialogic view of language, the product of his reading of Locke and his understanding of conversation, takes priority over his view that language and meaning are unified and pure, and it is expressed in the Preface to the *Dictionary*. In an elegiac tone appropriate to the loss of his Edenic conceptions, he realizes that

> *words are the daughters of earth, and that things are the sons of heaven.*
> Language is only the instrument of science, and words are but the signs of ideas: I wish, however, that the instrument might be less apt to decay, and that the signs might be permanent, like the things which they denote. (7)

Words, or language, decay with usage. Johnson wishes for permanence for both the sign and the ideas they represent, but he knows that this is impossible. Johnson realizes that one inquiry into the original meaning of a word only gives occasion to another, "that book referred to book, that to search was not always to find, and to find was not always to be informed; and that thus to pursue perfection, was . . . to chace the sun" (21). The search for truth or fixity, according to Johnson, is futile.

Defining words is difficult for Johnson, for he finds that "names . . . have often many ideas, but few ideas have many names" (15). To separate the meanings of single words is not always practical, for "kindred senses may be so interwoven, that the perplexity cannot be disentangled, nor any reason be assigned why one should be ranked before the other. . . . The shades of meaning sometimes pass imperceptibly into each other; so that though on one side they apparently differ, yet it is impossible to mark the point of contact" (15). The sense of mixing and interacting becomes apparent here. When it comes to defining meaning, words have no boundaries, so that their meanings bleed into each other, even when the reader is unaware. At the end of the Preface we get Johnson's final confession:

> Those who have been persuaded to think well of my design, require that it should fix our language, and put a stop to those alterations which time and chance have hither to been suffered to make in it without opposition. With this consequence I will confess that I flattered myself for a while; but now begin to fear that I have indulged expectation which neither reason nor experience can justify. (24)

This awareness, that neither "reason nor experience" justifies the belief that the decay of language can be stopped, is in Johnson's literary criticism used as the basis of many of his critical values. The instability of language implies that critical evaluation is also unstable — what is good art now may not be considered good art later. The problem is how to account for the shift of value in literary criticism. Johnson attempts to account for the shift by developing a rhetoric that reflects the flux and shift of conversation, where more than one point of view can be established. In the Preface to *The Works of William Shakespeare* (1765) Johnson takes the opportunity to question the classical values, which emphasize unity and transcendental truth, and to enter into a dialogic relationship with Shakespeare's prior editors.

The Menippean quality of the *Dictionary* is also found in the Preface to *Shakespeare*. Just as the juxtaposition of voices under each definition creates a Menippean quality in the *Dictionary,* so too does Johnson see the various editorial voices on Shakespeare's work in dialogue with each other. It is at this point that the definition of *voice* is expanded to include a point of view that sees the world in a particular way and evokes certain responses from other voices.[8] About one third of the Preface addresses the work of other Shakespearian editors, and Johnson places himself not in a superior position as Shakespeare's last editor, but in lateral position, because he sees the meaning of Shakespeare's texts cannot be fixed and that the interpretation of each play shifts from age to age.

Johnson discusses the work of each editor, what each has brought to the Shakespearian texts, and what he has taken from their work. He begins with Shakespeare's first editor, Rowe, who, Johnson relates, did not set out to correct or explain the texts, but to write "a life and recommendatory preface" (93). Rowe's concern as a critic was primarily biographical, and Johnson's criticism will distinguish itself from this. Pope is the next editor, and though Johnson has great reverence for him, he finds many faults in his work. Pope tried to reform the corruptness of Shakespeare's texts and "rejected whatever he disliked, and thought more of amputation than of cure" (94). Pope comes to represent the neoclassical critic who strives for unity and mimesis, and it is for this reason that Pope is preoccupied with the corruptness of Shakespeare's texts. Theobald, who followed Pope, is acknowledged by Johnson, though it is clear that Johnson has little respect for him. Theobald is "a man of narrow comprehension and small acquisitions, with no native and extrinsic splendour of genius, with little of the artificial light of learning, but zealous for minute accuracy, and not negligent in pursuing it" (95). Theobald is a pedant whom Johnson also hopes to distinguish himself from. The next editor is Sir Thomas Hammer, to whom Johnson attributes careful care of Shakespeare's meter, and from whom Johnson also borrows notes. But Johnson pays particular attention to his immediate predecessor, William Warburton. Johnson finds the predominant error of his commentary in his "acquiescence in his first thoughts" (98). That is, Warburton did not think through his initial responses, and therefore these responses are vague and undeveloped.

While writing about these various editors, Johnson is terribly conscious of himself and his editorial role, and he is careful to acknowledge the other editors, to show his audience his willingness to engage with them, while at the same time hoping to distinguish his project from theirs; it is the same kind of consciousness we find in the Preface to the *Dictionary*. Johnson sees the work of the critic as a process, and his articulation of this process is conveyed in the same melancholy tone he uses in the *Dictionary*:

> The opinions prevalent in one age, as truths above the reach of controversy, are confuted and rejected in another, and rise again to reception in remoter times. Thus the human mind is kept in motion without progress. . . . The tide of seeming knowledge which is poured over one generation retires and leaves another naked and barren; the sudden meteors of intelligence, which for a while appear to shoot their beams into the regions of obscurity, on a sudden withdraw their lustre, and leave mortals again to grope their way. (99)

What Johnson describes here is the process of literary history and the role of the critic in that history. As Johnson confutes the opinions of Shakespeare's previous critics, he realizes that with time his opinions will also be overturned.

The understanding that seems to be clear during one time becomes obscure in another. The flux and instability of language begin to have their implications for critical interpretations and the formation of literary history.

This is a process from which Johnson, himself, is not excluded:

> I had before my eyes so many critical adventures ended in miscarriage that caution was forced upon me. I encountered in every page Wit struggling with its own sophistry, and Learning confused by the multiplicity of its views. I was forced to censure those whom I admired, and could not but reflect, while I was dispossessing their emendations, how soon the same fate might happen to my own, and how many of the readings which I have corrected may be by some other editor defended and established. (109)

The fact that the meaning of single words, lines, or entire plays cannot be fixed is something Johnson is acutely aware of in his own writing. The act of displacing other voices to make room for his own is the very act of his own displacement. But it is the process of dialogue between editorial voices that is important for Johnson. What distinguishes his critical work is not only his awareness of the transitory nature of his opinion, but his articulation of this process and the placement of this articulation within the criticism itself. His literary criticism is not only the expression of value, but the description of process. He places his editorial voice, or point of view, in context with other editorial views, and we again see the Menippean characteristic, the juxtaposition of voice, being utilized. Instead of trying to displace the various editorial voices by ignoring or completely discounting them, he makes a place for himself, not by assuming his interpretation is the truest, but by allowing the other voices to become his own.

We find other Menippean qualities in the Preface.[9] Johnson praises Shakespeare for his ability to mix elements, thereby denoting a use of language that is fluid and not fixed. Those who adhered to classical rules saw Shakespeare's ability to mix high and low as his greatest fault. Johnson views Shakespeare's mixing of genres as what makes him so successful:

> Shakespeare's plays are not in the rigorous and critical sense either tragedies or comedies; but compositions of a distinct kind; exhibiting the real state of sublunary nature, which partakes of good and evil, joy and sorrow, mingled with endless variety of proportion and innumerable modes of combination; and expressing the course of the world, in which the loss of one is the gain of the other. (66)

Johnson appreciates Shakespeare's ability to create a dialogue between genres, and between each element in each genre so that we have a "distinct kind" of composition that portrays "the real state" of things. Johnson's experience allows him to see how knowledge is created through contrast and opposition. He knows the impossibility of stabilizing meaning and appreciates Shakespeare's ability to allow oppositions to exist simultaneously. Shakespeare unites disparate elements "not only in one mind but in one composition" (67), and he gives Johnson a method for understanding and expressing the particular kind of rhetoric he is trying to develop. Shakespeare and Johnson are, in fact, in dialogue with each other.

The psychological element of dialogue is described further in Johnson's analysis of Shakespeare. The value of mimesis that the eighteenth century upheld is redefined by Johnson. The "mirror of manners and life" (62) that Shakespeare holds up to his audience reveals dissonance and discord, a cacophony of social voices. Shakespeare's "mingled" drama approaches nearer than pure comedy or tragedy to "the appearance of life, by showing how great machinations and slender designs may promote or obviate one another, and the high and the low co-operate in the general system by unavoidable concatenation" (67). The psychological power of Shakespeare's drama comes from the fact that he always has an "interchange of seriousness and merriment, by which the mind is softened at one time, and exhilarated at another. . . . as he commands us, we laugh or mourn, or sit silent with quiet expectation, in tranquillity without indifference" (68). The reality that Shakespeare's work reflects is one of dialogue, where moods and emotions are constantly interacting with and affecting each other. The lesson Johnson learns about the nature of language and communication—that words do not signify reality and that knowledge is created through the interaction, or conversation, between varying points of view—is found in his literary commentary on Shakespeare.

In the Preface we can also see a dialogism emerging in Johnson's discourse.[10] Johnson writes with an absent auditor in mind, and it is this auditor who determines the structure of Johnson's argument. The absent interlocutors in Johnson's Preface are those who, like Pope, hold neoclassical values and believe that drama should adhere to the Aristotelian rules of genre and unities. Looking at the larger structure of Johnson's argument, we can see that he frames it in terms of dialogue. First, there are the "virtues" of Shakespeare's dramas, such as his "just representations of general nature" (61), and then there are the "faults sufficient to obscure and overwhelm any other merit" (71). Once Johnson has articulated these faults, he presents a third point of view, and this is directed to the classical critics:

> It will be thought strange that, in enumerating the defects of this
> writer, I have not yet mentioned his neglect of the unities; his vio-
> lation of those laws which have been instituted and established by
> the joint authority of poets and critics. (74-75)

Johnson acknowledges that Shakespeare has deviated from the classical
unities, and he claims that those laws have been established by the authority of neoclassical critics. These critics are distinguished from Johnson's
Common Reader, and it is for the Common Reader that he speaks. In an
impressive rhetorical thrust, which simultaneously respects and disregards
the critical tradition that precedes him, Johnson addresses the perspective
of the neoclassical critics: "But from the censure which this irregularity may
bring upon [Shakespeare], I shall, with due reverence to that learning
which I must oppose, adventure to try how I can defend him" (75). Johnson
respects the authority of the neoclassical critics because they are authorities,
and because they are authorities, he must speak up for the Common Reader.
He does so by describing the incongruities in Shakespeare's work, and
thereby encourages the subjective and individual interpretation.

Concerning the unity of action, Johnson argues that Shakespeare's plays
do, in fact, have "a beginning, a middle, and an end," and that "one event is
concatenated with another, and the conclusion follows by easy consequence"
(75). Toward the unities of time and place Johnson admits that Shakespeare
"has shown no regard" (75). But Johnson turns this statement by insisting
we look at the premise on which these rules exist. He states that the "necessity of observing the unities of time and place arises from the supposed
necessity of making the drama credible" (76). Credibility, for the neoclassical critic, means reality, and the reality that Shakespeare shows, according to Johnson, is full of discord and disparity.

Neoclassical critics believe if a play does not contain these unities the
"mind revolts from evident falsehood, and fiction loses its force when it
departs from the resemblance of reality" (76). Johnson believes that it is the
ability of literature to create an interaction with the mind and in the mind
that makes it successful. Plays produce "imitations" of actions in a sequence,
and changes in time are the easiest elements for the imagination to understand. The imitations of nature "produce pain or pleasure, not because they
are mistaken for realities, but because they bring realities to mind" (78).
What drama brings to the spectator is an experience and interaction with
the world; it is the processes of interaction and of creating knowledge that
make the dramatic works so realistic.

In a self-deprecating statement, Johnson anticipates the objections to his
argument, and at the same time he vindicates Shakespeare's lack of decorum.

> Yet when I speak thus slightly of dramatic rules, I cannot but recollect how much wit and learning may be produced against me; before such authorities I am afraid to stand, not that I think the present question one of those that are to be decided by mere authority, but because it is to be suspected that these precepts have not been so easily received but for better reasons than I have yet been able to find. . . . the unities of time and place are not essential to a just drama. (80)

Johnson's rhetoric is used to redefine dramatic action. He constructs a dialogue between the neoclassical critics and not himself, but a rhetorical position or point of view. What at first appears to be a single voiced or monologic discourse is, in fact, dialogic, and its split structure creates the knowledge that is its content.

The influence of Johnson's notions of language and meaning are also found in the *Lives of the English Poets* (1781-89). A discussion of the dialogical nature of Johnson's *Lives* can begin with an analysis of literary biography. The Menippean quality of mixing genre that Johnson praises Shakespeare for distinguishes Johnson's own writing. As Lawrence Lipking points out, "No study of the *Lives* can be convincing unless it confronts their *lack* of any obvious unity, their formal variety, their passages of hackwork, their ability to please readers whose definitions have nothing to do with each other" (409). Lipking describes five generic types that the *Lives* contain. The *Lives* are: 1) literary criticism both practical and theoretical; 2) biography; 3) prefaces to a definitive anthology of English poetry; 4) literary and intellectual history, as well as documents in that history; and 5) moral and psychological observations, with affinities both to the periodical essay and to the Theophrastan character (Lipking 456). The *Lives* are not limited to these types, nor are they purely one type or another. Instead, each *Life* is some combination of all five. The *Lives* deal with the life and work of each author, but come to no formal solution to the structural relation between them.

Though the mixture of biography and criticism is one with which twentieth-century readers are familiar, Johnson's innovation is his use of different types of discourse, such as those Lipking delineates, as a means of understanding a writer. Johnson's point of view may be essentially monological, but the dialogic also embraces the merging of discourses, and it is this merging that allows us to view the subject from a perspective other than a single discourse would allow. He is proficient at each genre—biography and literary criticism, for example—and he filters one through the other so that they interact and help to give meaning to each other. This interaction gives a more realistic view of each life, just as Shakespeare's mixed dramas gave a more realistic view of the world.

The "Life of Gray" sets up this kind of dialogic relation between the life and work of the author. Of Gray's character Johnson attributes "common sense," which is pleasing, according to Johnson, to all men. By appealing to common sense, Gray appeals to what is common in all men; he does not limit his writing to what only the authoritative critic would understand. Common sense allows the Common Reader to interpret and experience the writing for himself. When reading Gray's letters the Common Reader finds that Gray's "contempt . . . is often employed, where I hope it will be approved, upon skepticism and infidelity" (III: 432). For Johnson, it is good sense to reject skepticism. But, though Gray has common sense, and though he rejects skepticism, the fault of Gray's poetry is that is lacks "sense."

In Gray's poem on the cat, "Selima, the cat, is called a nymph, with some violence both to sound and sense . . ." (III: 434). The emphasis here is on the "sense" of the poetry, where the poem's content offends the "sense" of the reader because it does not make "sense." Johnson also finds Gray's poem, "The Bard," fallacious for the same reason. In it his "stanzas are too long, especially his epodes; the ode is finished before the ear has learned its measures, and, consequently, before it can receive pleasure from their consonance and recurrence" (III: 438-39). The "sense" of the poem is directly related to its sound, and because the sound and form are not clear, neither is the "sense" the poem attempts to explain.

The famous passage from this "Life," the passage that Woolf quotes in the introduction to *The Common Reader*, praises Gray's "Elegy" because of the effect it has on the "sense" of the reader:

> I rejoice to concur with the common reader; for, by the common sense of readers uncorrupted with literary prejudices, after all the refinements of subtlety and the dogmatism of learning, must be finally decided all claim to poetical honours. The churchyard abounds with images which find a mirror in every mind, and with sentiments to which every bosom returns an echo. (III: 441)

The Common Reader who responds to literature with his common sense is the reader with whom Johnson identifies. Gray's "Elegy" contains images that mirror the experience of the reader, and it contains sentiments that every reader echoes in dialogue with the writer. "Sense" and all its possible connotations become the object of the internal dialogue with which Johnson structures the essay; Gray's success or failure is based on his ability to appeal to the different kinds of "sense," whether it is "sense" in terms of meaning or "sense" in terms of sensibility.

In contrast, Dryden's life and work are bound by "ratiocination." His is a poetry of ideas, not images. He is the "father of English criticism" (I: 410) and, therefore, a poet and critic to whom Johnson owes reverence. In describing Dryden's work, Johnson is describing his own. The absent interlocutor to whom Johnson is speaking is he who would attack the critic who is also a poet and the style of his criticism. We find Johnson defining . Dryden as a poet: "[T]he criticism of Dryden is the criticism of a poet; not a dull collection of theorems, but a gay and vigorous dissertation, where delight is mingled with instruction, and where the author proves his right of judgement by his power of performance" (I: 412). What we have in Dryden is the dialogic mixing of poetry and prose, of "delight" and "instruction." Dryden is the first critic to use a poetic diction in criticism and to use criticism in poetic diction. The dialogic nature of Dryden's discourse is found in his intermingling of high and low.

Johnson pursues his discussion of the mixed nature of Dryden's language, and it reminds us of his statements on Shakespeare's mixing of genres: "Every language of a learned nation necessarily divides itself into diction scholastick and popular, grave and familiar, elegant and gross: and from a nice distinction of these different parts arises a great part of the beauty of style" (I: 420). Before the time of Dryden there was "no poetical diction, no system of words at once refined from the grossness of domestick use, and free from the harshness of terms appropriated to particular arts" (I: 420). Dryden mixes the language of poetry into the language of criticism and, like Johnson, he mediates the two genres. Johnson believes "Words too familiar, or too remote, defeat the purpose of a poet" (I: 420), and Dryden manages to combine both, to use them in an interactive relation to each other. According to Johnson, Dryden is responsible for the merging of high and low in poetry and criticism, giving the vulgar quality of prose a poetic texture. Dryden allows the attributes of one discourse to inform the other, just as Johnson is doing in his own literary criticism.

Alexander Pope, on the other hand, is noted for his "poetical prudence." The most penetrating description of Pope is found in Johnson's comparison of him to Dryden. Johnson's language echoes his previously quoted passage on the difference between speaking and writing; Dryden and Pope are distinguished by qualities of expansion and constriction.

> Dryden's performances were always hasty, either excited by some external occasion, or extorted by domestick necessity; he composed without consideration, and published without correction.
> . . . The dilatory caution of Pope enabled him to condense his sentiments, to multiply his images, and to accumulate all that study

might produce, or chance might supply. If the flights of Dryden, therefore, are higher, Pope continues longer on the wing. If of Dryden's fire the blaze is brighter, of Pope's heat is more regular and constant. Dryden often surpasses expectation, and Pope never falls below it. Dryden is read with frequent astonishment, and Pope with perpetual delight. (III: 223)

The parallel Johnson draws between Dryden and Pope is not just a comparison and contrast of the two writers. The constructions are not conditional but dialogic in that the value of each writer is determined by the other. Pope's "longer" flight is dependent on Dryden's "higher" one; his "regular and constant" heat on Dryden's "brighter" fire; his affect of "perpetual delight" on Dryden's "frequent astonishment." The elements in these comparisons are not mutually exclusive but mutually dependent. Johnson uses the same similes to describe them, but emphasizes different connotations. The shared figures make the two writers similar, yet different. Their importance and qualities merge and mix with each other, and the meanings "converse," allowing us to understand one in terms of the other. Johnson creates two semantic points of view with his descriptions of Dryden and Pope, and with these points of view he creates a conversation or dialogue that gives a sense of what each writer can and cannot do.

Johnson's two most famous *Lives*, the "Life of Cowley" and the "Life of Milton," also contain the same dialogical elements. It is in relation to these two poets that we sense Johnson's greatest conflict, and the greater the conflict, the stronger his use of the dialogical method.

In the "Life of Cowley," Johnson is most critical of the breed of poets he terms "metaphysical." It is curious that he attacks them on the level of style, a style that in many ways, according to the present study, resembles his own. The goal of the metaphysical poets, in Johnson's view, is to demonstrate wit, "to show their learning was their whole endeavor" (I: 19). The problem with the metaphysicals is that wit for them is "rigorously and philosophically considered as a kind of 'discordia concors,' a combination of dissimilar images, or of occult resemblances in things apparently unlike" (I: 20). Wit of this kind, Johnson says, they have enough. In their poetry the

most heterogeneous ideas are yoked by violence together; nature and art ransacked for illustrations, comparisons, and allusions; their learning instructs, and their subtlety surprises; but the reader commonly thinks his improvement dearly bought, and, though he sometimes admires, is seldom pleased. (I: 20)

Johnson's definition of seventeenth-century wit is of one who uses conversation the wrong way. The learning of the metaphysical poet is too arcane and abrupt for the Common Reader to obtain any knowledge. The "heterogeneous" ideas are pulled together in a violent and unsystematic way. The learning the Common Reader receives is achieved through an arduous process that does not allow for the kind of interaction she looks for.

Though the metaphysicals failed as a whole, Cowley is the best. But what Cowley and the others lack is an understanding of how language works as a dialogical system, an understanding that Johnson gained while writing his dictionary. Johnson's is a corrective statement, showing how Cowley and the others go astray in their dialogical notion of knowledge. The poets seemed "not to have known, or not to have considered, that words, being arbitrary, must owe their power to association, and have the influence, and that only, which custom gives them" (I: 55). Johnson is here describing the social elements of language: the way in which the meaning of one word is the function of another, and how usage in a certain context by certain speakers determines many of a word's possible connotations. Meaning is "arbitrary," and only "custom" or social agreement gives stability to language. It is the lack of such a conception of language that prevents the metaphysical poets from communicating their knowledge. Because of their misuse of language, the wits' ideas are so buried as not to be worth "the cost of their extraction" (I: 55).

Milton is the writer who causes Johnson the most anxiety. Usually, Johnson's language shows a reverence for Milton, but it is often tainted with severe criticism. It is important to remember that in Johnson's work, interaction, contradiction, opposition, and conflict—in essence, conversation and dialogue—are the grounding from which knowledge emerges. Like the Preface to *Shakespeare*, the structure of the "Life of Milton" implies the awareness of an interlocutor. However, this essay reveals two interlocutors, and they are not absent but present in the discourse, perpetually responding and interacting with each other. If we assume that these voices are Johnson's, we must acknowledge that his opinion vacillates throughout the text, and that he often appears to contradict himself.

The voices that Johnson sets up in the essay have two distinct connotations. The first speaks of pollution, contamination, lies, imagination, skepticism, and science. The language of the other voice alludes to cleanliness, truth, fact, reason, common sense, and morality. These two voices merge and separate throughout the work, and it is often difficult to ascertain Johnson's final evaluation; and so we must decide that it is not the evaluation that is most important, but the process by which that evaluation is determined.

In the first part of the "Life of Milton," Johnson describes Milton as an educator, and Johnson uses this as an opportunity to articulate the view of education against which Milton will be judged:

> Whether we provide for action or conversation, whether we wish to be useful or pleasing, the first requisite is the religious and moral knowledge of right and wrong; the next is the acquaintance with the history of mankind, and with those examples which may be said to embody truth, and prove, by events, the reasonableness of opinions. (I: 99-100)

Here we have stated the criteria by which Johnson will evaluate Milton. Science, which leads to skepticism, is not an appropriate exercise of the mind and is therefore not the appropriate material for poetry. The function of education and poetry is to teach "religious and moral knowledge of right and wrong" and the "history of mankind" that serves as exemplum for reasonable behavior. This can be achieved through the dialogic interaction that would allow the reader to apply his common sense.

It is the point of view of "religious and moral knowledge" that is found and contrasted in Johnson's analysis of "Lycidas." In the poem, "the diction is harsh, the rhymes uncertain, and the numbers unpleasing." Therefore, "what beauty there is, we must . . . seek in the sentiments and images" (I: 163). But of the images Johnson finds, "there is no nature, for there is no truth; there is no art, for there is nothing new" (I: 163). He accuses Milton of mixing good values with bad ones: "With these trifling fictions are mingled the most awful and sacred truths, such as ought never to be polluted with such irreverent combinations" (I: 165). There is "no truth" to be found in the images, yet the truths are "sacred"; the "beauty" is in the images, not in the diction, though there is no "art" to be found in the poetry at all. It is clear that Johnson does not approve of "Lycidas," but why he does not approve is more obscure. The critical language he uses to describe the poem is not stable; we are not sure what he means when he uses the terms "nature," "truth," "beauty," "sacred," and "art." The meaning and value of these terms mingle and cross boundaries, and so every reader of Johnson and "Lycidas" is forced to interpret Johnson's criticism for himself. Instead of turning to the authority of the critic, the reader turns to his own experience of Milton, his own common sense, to judge the success or failure of Milton's work. Johnson appreciates "L'Allegro" and "Il Penseroso" because the form and structure of the poems allow meaning to be fluid and unstable. The poems show how "among the successive variety of appearances, every disposition of mind takes hold on those by which it might be gratified" (I: 166). Milton portrays contrasting states within the mind of one reader—the two poems gain their fullest meaning when viewed in relation to each other, that is, as a dialogue of two voices.

The climax of Johnson's essay is in his discussion of *Paradise Lost*. Here, the values Johnson previously said should not be mixed—reason and imagination—are successfully brought together. Johnson defines poetry as "the art of uniting pleasure with truth, by calling imagination to the help of reason" (I: 170). The epic poem teaches "the most important truths by the most pleasing precepts" (I: 170), and therefore Milton relates an important moral and a great event in the most effective way.

Milton's greatest quality is his sublimity, and the sublime element of his poetry lies in his ability to astonish. He astonishes, according to Johnson, because he "never fails to fill the imagination" (I: 178). There is a qualification, however, for his "images and descriptions of the scenes, or operations of nature, do not seem to be always copied from original form, nor have the freshness, raciness, and energy of immediate observation" (I: 178).

The images Milton uses do not come from real life, and so it is difficult for the reader to identify, interact, and interpret them. The greatest criticism of *Paradise Lost* is that it "comprises neither human actions nor human manners" (I: 181). The reader finds "no transaction in which he can be engaged; beholds no condition in which he can, by any effort of imagination, place himself; he has, therefore, little natural curiosity or sympathy" (I: 181). The ability to "astonish" is lacking in this description; it is Milton's inability to engage the mind that Johnson addresses.

There is then another turn in the essay as the analysis describes Milton's ability to "select from nature or from story, from ancient fable or from modern science, whatever could illustrate or adorn his thoughts" (I: 183). An "accumulation of knowledge impregnated" Milton's mind, "fermented by study, and exalted by imagination" (I: 183). Again, though, there is a "want of human interest" in Milton's work. And it is in the following passage that we sense Johnson's problematic relationship with Milton:

> *Paradise Lost* is one of the books which the reader admires and lays down, and forgets to take up again. None ever wished it longer than it is. Its perusal is a duty rather than a pleasure. We read Milton for instruction, retire harassed and overburdened, and look elsewhere for recreation; we desert our master, and seek for companions. (I: 183-84)

Johnson, as reader of *Paradise Lost*, expresses the problematic relationship he has with a writer who is as rigorous and vital in his dialogue with his readers as Johnson is. It is the same kind of antagonistic relationship that Leslie Stephen has with Johnson. What Milton shows the reader, as the reader compares what he reads to his own experience, are difficult elements of human existence. On the other hand, the reader, in order to overcome the burdensome reading Milton gives him, must develop a reading of his experience that overrides Milton's. Because of Milton's strength as a reader and writer, this is almost impossible for the reader, including Johnson, to do. Instead, Johnson turns to those he can have a more congenial dialogue with. But this is disingenuous on Johnson's part, because he often tries to dominate writers and readers weaker than himself.

With Johnson's dialogic rhetoric, which is split in its intention and meaning, he brings the disparate elements of his essay together in his final statement on Milton. Milton, "like other heroes . . . is to be admired rather than imitated" (I: 194). We should be engaged by Milton, but we are not, and this lack of engagement is for the very reason that his poetry does everything it is supposed to do — Milton's accomplishment is too much to tolerate.

In the "Life of Milton," we find the greatest tension between critical values that Johnson strains to pull together. What he tells us about Milton's poetry is a function of the opposition he creates when discussing it. In his criticism of *Paradise Lost*, Johnson praises Milton for being able to bring reason and imagination together. The mixing of truth and fiction is the basis for his criticism of "Lycidas." In this analysis we find not only the interchange of values in Johnson's critical vocabulary, but also an interchange in the *application* of those values. We might construe this as a contradiction on Johnson's part, but consistency implies a unified and fixed meaning. Milton, in fact, does exactly what Johnson describes — he mixes fiction and truth, and he doesn't mix fiction and truth, and it is Milton's ability to do this that causes Johnson so much anxiety.

Milton has the ability to merge fact and fiction through difference and opposition in a way that Johnson is unable to do. Johnson attempts this same kind of technique in his fictional work, *Rasselas* (1759). In this work we find the application of a dialogical technique, though crude in its development, reflecting the beginning of what will later develop into the sophisticated narrative of Virginia Woolf's later novels. Johnson's *Rasselas*, written after the *Dictionary* but before *Shakespeare* and the *Lives*, serves as the best example of a technique and conception of language that has been transferred into twentieth-century prose fiction. This discussion of Johnson's dialogical conception of language will end with an analysis of *Rasselas* because it is his only attempt to represent aesthetically the notion of dialogue and conversation.[11]

Rasselas is the representation of an idea. In this sense the idea is "inter-individual and inter-subjective — the realm of existence is not individual consciousness but dialogic communion *between* consciousnesses. . . . In this sense the idea is like the *word*. . . . like the word, the idea wants to be heard, understood, and 'answered' by other voices from other positions. . . . the idea is by nature dialogic" (*PDP* 88). Johnson's *Rasselas* is the artistic construction of the *idea*, and the idea's life is found in dialogue.

On a literal level, *Rasselas* contains one dialogue after another. Chapter titles include "A Dissertation on the Art of Flying"; "Imlac's Narrative Continued"; "The Princess Continues her Remarks upon Private Life"; "Rasselas and Nekayah Continue their Conversation"; "The Debate on Marriage Continued"; and "Imlac Enters and Changes the Conversation." There are few descriptive passages, no real plot, nor any omniscient narrator giving us information the characters are unaware of.

The didactic element of dialogue is found in the relationship between the characters as they constantly teach and learn from each other. In an effort to determine what "choice of life" he wants, Rasselas exchanges words. In the happy valley he talks with his teacher, the scientist of the "flying chair," and, most importantly, with Imlac. After he leaves the valley he speaks with a variety of personages, including the "young men of spirit and gaiety," the "wise and happy man," the hermit, men of high station, and the "man of learning," not to mention the chapters devoted to his conversations with his sister Nekayah on subjects such as marriage and mourning.

The enunciations of each speaker share a common object, the idea of "earthly happiness." We are reminded of *Idler* No. 85 in which Johnson describes the necessity of a man of learning to mix with mankind in order to complete his knowledge. He must come into contact with men who "placed in various situations view the same object on many sides" (II: 415), and he must gain through experience the power "of changing a position into various forms" (II: 415). "Diversity" is the dominant rhetorical figure in *Rasselas*. We are given diverse points of view on the idea that there is no earthly happiness, as well as the equation between Rasselas's quest to choose a life and his quest for diversity.

What Rasselas desires is a sense of diversity and difference; in the happy valley he "wants" nothing and knows not what he "wants": every hour and every day seem like every other. He longs to see "the miseries of the world, since the sight of them is necessary to happiness" (16). In order to know what he has, he must see what he has not. He wishes to "mingle with mankind" (18) to get a sense of who and what he is.

Other themes are represented with dialogical configurations. For example, the origin of love between young people is found in dialogue: "'A youth and a maiden meeting by chance, or brought together by artifice, exchange glances, reciprocate civilities, go home, and dream of one another'" (107). However, this kind of interaction is not complete, so neither is the love that they experience: "'Having little to divert attention, or diversify thought, they find themselves uneasy when they are apart, and therefore conclude they shall be happy together'" (107). This conclusion is not necessarily accurate, especially since young people don't have the diversity of thought and experience to add to their knowledge.

The creative thinker also suffers from a lack of diversity. The astronomer, a learned man who has isolated himself for his science, succumbs to the dangers of imagination—he deludes himself into thinking he controls the weather. But after spending much time socializing and conversing with Rasselas, Nekayah, and Imlac, he begins to regain his senses. He comments on his isolated existence to his companions: "'I have, since my thoughts have been diversified by more intercourse with the world, begun to question the reality" (161). It is the unreality of solitude that he questions. And by the end of the conversation, Rasselas, too, believes that "'variety . . . is so necessary to content that even the happy valley disgusted me by the recurrence of its luxuries . . .'" (164). This is not the first time Rasselas has learned this lesson. What we find is Rasselas's unwillingness to accept diversity, flux, and change as the truth he's been searching for.

It is in Rasselas's conversation with Imlac that he gets a firm sense of his need to see perspectives other than his own. When Imlac gives his history, he says that the life he devoted to learning and knowledge was "very little diversified by events" (31). Because of this he has left the world of scholarly existence to enter the world of human experience and interaction. For a poet, this kind of experience is essential:

> "But the knowledge of nature is only half the task of the poet; he must be acquainted likewise with all the modes of life. His character requires that he estimate the happiness and misery of every condition; observe all the power of all the passions in their combinations, and trace the changes of the human mind as they are modified by various institutions and accidental influences of climate or custom." (44)

Poetic knowledge is based on a dialogue among "modes of life," passions in their combinations, "changes of the human mind," and various institutions. The poet, according to Johnson, has the sensibility that is most perceptive to diversity because he takes in all aspects of experience.

After talking with Imlac, Rasselas recognizes the need to "mingle with this mighty confluence of nations," and how little his life has made him "acquainted with the diversity of opinions" (47). Imlac becomes the guide for Rasselas and his sister, Nekayah, and he leads them into the world of diversity and difference. Within the first few days of leaving the happy valley, Imlac becomes "diverted with the admiration which his companions expressed at the diversity of manners, stations, and employments" (62). Imlac prepares "to set before them the various ranks and conditions of mankind," so that they each can make their "choice of life" (63). But the key to Rasselas's quest is answered by Imlac about halfway through their travels:

> "The causes of good and evil," answered Imlac, "are so various and uncertain, so often entangled with each other, so diversified by various relations, and so much subject to accidents which cannot be foreseen that he who would fix his condition upon uncontestable reasons of preference, must live and die inquiring and deliberating." (67)

This is the nature of knowledge, not only in Rasselas's search, but also in the discourse through which Rasselas's experience is represented. The "good" and "evil" choices represented in this narrative are so "entangled" and dependent on each other for their meaning that he who tries to find one originating event upon which to base an interpretation will be perpetually dissatisfied. Like Rasselas, who ignores Imlac's advice and who cannot see that Imlac is giving him the very information he is looking for, the reader who looks for closure in the work—that is, looks for a unified and singular meaning—will be as blind as Rasselas in finding the truth.

The narrative ends with the chapter entitled, "The Conclusion, in Which Nothing is Concluded." Rasselas has been participating in the kind of activity that Imlac claims has given him diversity of thought, conversation, and intercourse with other men. The last scene is of Rasselas and his company in conversation: "and being well supplied with materials for talk, they diverted themselves with comparisons of the different forms of life which they had observed, and with various schemes of happiness which each of them had formed" (175). It is not surprising that they should choose to return to the happy valley. Though the conversers may not be aware of it, they have gained a diversity of experience and point of view that allows them to mix ideas and images in their own minds, and therefore they return to their homes with different perspectives.

What we find in *Rasselas* is a representation of the theories of language and meaning that Johnson articulates in his *Dictionary* and later utilizes in

Shakespeare and the *Lives*. Not only is *Rasselas* virtually one conversation after another, but the idea of diversity and difference, and the function of difference in them, help Rasselas to know what he wants. In the last scene it is the diversity of voices and interpretations of the meaning of life that is most evident; and it is this cacophony of voices that constitutes meaning in *Rasselas*. Those who read Johnson as a moral and didactic writer find *Rasselas* flawed, for it is impossible to pull one unified meaning from the text. If we read Johnson as a dialogist, then the value of *Rasselas* is heightened because of the same inability to retrieve a single interpretation.

A century after Johnson's writing, Leslie Stephen approached Johnson's work with a theoretically unified perspective and praised Johnson for his sense of social responsibility. However, he found Johnson's writing style and rhetorical techniques greatly flawed. Virginia Woolf reacts against her father by adopting Johnson as her literary father and reading him antithetically from Stephen, as a dialogist. The use of conversation and voices found in *Rasselas* bears an unusual likeness, though crude and underdeveloped in this work, to Woolf's essays and novels.

◆3◆

Virginia Woolf and Samuel Johnson:
Conversation and the Common Reader

There is a conservative element in Virginia Woolf's criticism that reminds us of Leslie Stephen, his construction of Samuel Johnson, and his desire to place moral and social responsibilities on the critic and writer.[1] Woolf, however, is not quite as bound to those critical precepts as her father, and she is constantly taking risks, developing innovative notions of literary history, and concentrating less on the didactic function of a writer than on the reader herself and how the reader learns to read and to construct knowledge without the help of the critic. Because Woolf lacks Johnson's explicit moral and didactic quality, it is difficult to understand how he influenced her.

In investigating the influence of Johnson on Woolf we find there is more than just Woolf's casual reference to the Common Reader. First, Woolf directly alludes to Johnson in at least twenty-six essays.[2] Her reading notebooks show that she appealed to Johnson as an authority when she researched her early essays and articles. In a review of an edition of the *Life of Johnson*, Woolf speaks of Johnson in the superlative, naming him the "Saint Samuel" who has "proved himself of the stuff that saints and miracle workers are made of."[3] She also quotes a passage from the "Life of Milton," and states that it is cited by other commentators as one example of the "great critic's aberrations" in his writing style, an example of what others called the "Johnsonian incubus." But for Woolf the passage that she quotes is an example of the "grace and elasticity of his style," a style that, in many ways, Woolf tries to emulate. From this small review essay, which says more about the edition of the *Life of Johnson* than Johnson himself, and her many brief allusions to her precursor throughout her critical work, Woolf's regard and admiration for Johnson are quite clear.

Woolf's reverence for Johnson emerges in essay after essay. While describing the London streets, she asks her readers to "recall what Dr. Johnson said about Charing Cross," assuming her readers, like herself, recall his every word ("The Stranger" 201). But more typically, Woolf alludes to Johnson when she is trying to establish the value of another writer, either by comparing him to Johnson or by evoking Johnson's opinion about that writer. For example, in her essay "A Man with a View," she describes Samuel Butler as a man in the same company as Johnson. Both Butler and Johnson are "one of those rare spirits among the dead whom we like, or it may be dislike, as we do the living, so strong is their individuality and so clearly can we make up our minds about their manners and opinions" (28). Here Woolf testifies to the strength of Johnson's character and personality. Whether she uses him to support her readings or whether she disagrees with him, she does not deny the overwhelming presence of Johnson in her reading experience.

To establish the authority and stature of the Bluestocking Elizabeth Carter, Woolf cites Johnson who "appointed Carter to be Archbishop of Canterbury—" when it was proposed to form a government of women. For, Johnson stated, "'who is there . . . that [she] cannot influence?'" ("The Bluest" 113). In the same way, Woolf cites Johnson on another important female intellectual, Mrs. Montagu. Woolf tells us that "it is charitable to remember, before we form our verdict, that Johnson said of the author: 'she diffuses more knowledge in her conversation than any woman I know or, indeed, almost any man'" ("Passing Hour" 62).

A minor and obscure figure like Giuseppi Baretti finds legitimacy in Woolf's writing because of Johnson. Johnson stated that he "knows no man who carries his head higher in conversation than Baretti" ("A Friend" 188). Woolf tells us that the "merits of the society which Johnson ruled were precisely to the taste of Baretti" (188) and that Baretti tried to emulate Johnson's behavior. His success or failure is based on his ability to do what Johnson did and to evoke the same responses Johnson evoked.

This does not mean that Woolf always agreed with Johnson. In discussing Patmore's writing, she compares it to Johnson's:

> Placed directly after one of Johnson's Lives of the Poets one of Patmore's essays can be read, so far as the diction goes, without any of that gradual loosening of the attention which attacks us as prose weakens under the adulteration of unnecessary words, slack cadences, and worn-out metaphors. ("Patmore's Criticism" 36)

Yet, Woolf's comments on Johnson's style are not completely disapproving, nor does she view Patmore as Johnson's equal:

> [W]e shall somehow gather the impression that while Johnson is constantly outrageous and Patmore almost invariably civilized, Johnson's papers are the small visible fragment of a monster, Mr. Patmore's essays have about them no such suggestion of unexpressed magnitude. (36)

Woolf finds the same kind of power and awe in Johnson as Leslie Stephen did. Johnson's prose is "outrageous" and is only a fragment of his thought and expression, which is described in terms of a nightmarish figure of a "monster."

Stronger disapproval of Johnson is found in Woolf's essay, "Congreve's Comedies". According to Woolf, it was Congreve who "incurred first the majestic censure of Dr. Johnson" (36). This is because Congreve offended Johnson with some of his coarse scenes. But Woolf disagrees: "On the contrary [to Johnson], to read Congreve's plays is to be convinced that we may learn from them many lessons much to our advantage both as writers of books and . . . livers of life" (36). She believes that "to agree with Dr. Johnson is an impossibility. To read the comedies is not to 'relax those obligations by which life ought to be regulated.' On the contrary, the more slowly we read him and the more carefully, the more meaning we find, the more beauty we discover" (40).

Johnson, for Woolf, is a worthy opponent, and disagreements like the one she has over Congreve only reinforce our view of her regard for him. She shares with Stephen an antagonistic relationship with their common literary father. Johnson, with Coleridge and Dryden, is among the three great critics, and though she encourages readers to understand literature through their own experience, this experience can also help us to understand Johnson's greatness. For through our own reading we construct our own questions and suggestions, and only then can we approach a critic like Johnson without being like "a sheep in the shade of a hedge" ("How Should One Read" 244). A critic like Johnson, in his "considered criticism," is often "surprisingly relevant" for he can "light up and solidify the vague ideas that have been tumbling in the misty depths of our minds" (244).

The more substantial relation between Woolf and Johnson adumbrated above can be traced through Leslie Stephen, who trained his daughter in the art of criticism. There has been significant work done on Woolf's relation to Stephen, but Katherine C. Hill's study presents in detail Woolf's psychological "identification" with Stephen as he mentored her in literary criticism.[4] Stephen not only served as her model for writing but also for reading; though Woolf might not have always agreed with her father's critical assumptions and evaluations, she was certainly aware of them.

Besides serving as the commissioned editor of the *Dictionary of National Biography* from 1885 to 1901 and as the editor of *Cornhill Magazine,* to which he contributed many of his own essays, Stephen wrote numerous works on eighteenth-century thought and literature, including *English Thought in the Eighteenth Century* (1876), *English Literature and Society in the Eighteenth Century* (1904), and a full-length biography, *Samuel Johnson* (1900). Stephen was influential in the movement, occurring during the end of the nineteenth century, to recuperate and reevaluate the work of eighteenth-century writers and thinkers. Johnson's influence on Stephen, though not always congenial, was considerable. Woolf read the work of both her father and Johnson, and her reading of Johnson can be viewed as a function of her father's influence. The many studies of Stephen's influence on Woolf have focused on the biographical, psychological, intellectual, and literary perspectives.[5] None, however, concentrates on how this influence manifests itself in Woolf's reading and writing strategies.

Stephen, unlike his daughter, finds no way to read Johnson that will help him to defeat Johnson's overwhelming critical presence. The only way he can protect himself from being completely overshadowed is by limiting his understanding to that of Johnson as a great moralist and personality rather than focusing on the way Johnson allows his conversation to be integrated into his writing. Woolf, on the other hand, misreads Johnson in a positive and healthy way: she explores the nuances and implications of his writing to their fullest extent, and eventually exploits what she learns from him to turn on her literary mentor, Leslie Stephen, and their mutual literary influence, Johnson himself.

Stephen and Woolf represent two different yet simultaneous readings of Johnson. As an eighteenth-century critic and scholar, Johnson is traditionally seen in a neoclassical tradition, but he also moves away from the neoclassical tradition and the authority it propounds. As W. J. Bate points out, Johnson takes the classical values and vocabulary and gives them flexibility and elasticity so that their functions incorporate new, expanded meanings.[6] Johnson begins his career with the intention of upholding the classical values, seeing them as able to represent universal truths about human nature and art and bringing a coherent vision to the world. By the time Johnson had completed the *Dictionary*, he saw that shades of meaning pass imperceptively into each other and that it is impossible to distinguish boundaries. Meaning, for the experienced Johnson, is no longer something that is located in language itself, but is found in dialogue, the interaction and relation between simultaneous differences.

It is this later Johnson whom Woolf reads. Her reading of Johnson is one that sees the rules of literature as fluid and not limited to the structures of classical paradigms, where meaning is found in process and interaction. It is important, however, to understand that Johnson's criticism contains both the classical and dialogic criteria for judging literature, and that neither reading is privileged over the other. Both are a function of the strategies with which Stephen and Woolf approach him.

For Woolf, Johnson does not see art and nature as fixed entities with determinate characteristics. The value of a work of art is based on its ability to evoke a response in that audience.[7] This audience has the ability to react, respond, judge, and submit to experience (Damrosch 102). The Common Reader, the reading process, and the psychological approach to literary criticism are concerns both Virginia Woolf and Samuel Johnson pursue through their critical work. As critics, Woolf and Johnson abdicate their responsibility, giving it instead to their individual readers. And it is only in the reading process, the interaction and dialogue between reader and text, that meaning is created.

We see Johnson's influence on Woolf's critical thinking in her essay, "Hours in a Library," titled after her father's collection of essays. In this essay Woolf echoes the famous passage from Johnson's "Life of Gray":

> I rejoice to concur with the common reader; for, by the common sense of readers uncorrupted with literary prejudices, after all the refinements of subtlety and dogmatism of learning, must be finally decided all claim to poetical honours. (Johnson, *Lives* 487)

In her essay, Woolf, like Johnson, distinguishes between two types of readers: the Common Reader and the critic. She states that a reader must check his desire for learning at the outset, for "if knowledge sticks to him well and good, but to go in pursuit of it, to read on a system, to become a specialist or an authority, is very apt to kill what suits us to consider the more human passion for pure and disinterested reading" (34). Woolf warns against the tendency toward dogmatism in our knowledge of literature. It is the quality of spontaneity and the ability to allow literature to affect us that Woolf and Johnson endorse in their reader.

This is not to say that Woolf falls into the "aesthetic skepticism" her father warns against, where all taste is subjective and arbitrary. Woolf sees that there is a reason why classics have endured through time: "New books may be more stimulating and in some ways more suggestive then the old, but they do not give us that absolute certainty of delight which breathes through us" (39). Classics endure, not because there is something inherently more true or pure about them, but because they continue to evoke responses in their readers.

Unlike her father, who believes only the critic is capable of making distinctions for the vulgar and ignorant because he has a responsibility to propagate moral behavior, Woolf sees the Common Reader as capable of making these distinctions for him- or herself. This is why it is important for the reader to experience the classics: whatever we have learned "from reading the classics we need now in order to judge the work of our contemporaries, for whenever there is life in them they will be casting their net out over some unknown abyss to snare new shapes, and we must throw our imaginations after them if we are to accept with understanding the strange gifts they bring back to us" (39). Reading the classics helps the individual reader to develop an imagination and therefore contributes to better understanding and judgement of contemporary writers. And, in a reciprocal relation, we require the contemporaries for our reading of the classics, for "if we need all our knowledge of the old writers in order to follow what the new writers are attempting, it is certainly true that we come from adventuring among new books with a far keener eye for the old" (39). To determine the value and meaning of the classics and contemporaries we must read them in relation to each other and allow them to come into dialogue, to be known through their similarities and differences. In this way the reader's response, deepened by comparison, contrast, and self-consciousness, expands and reflects upon itself.[8]

Thus what begins in Johnson as neoclassicism redefined, with notions of art and nature having the ability to evoke responses in the viewer or reader, becomes in Woolf a criticism in which the reader's relationship to a text is inseparable from its meaning. Woolf values the reader's ability to respond to a piece of writing, and her critic is also an individual or Common Reader. But unlike her father, who sees the Common Reader and critic as having separate reading strategies, she sees the Common Reader as a critic who must trust his experience of the classics. That experience is used as a touchstone for judging contemporaries, even as contemporaries serve as a touchstone for judging the classics.

The Common Reader becomes an important agency in Woolf's criticism, and many scholars of Woolf's essays have attempted to understand and define the qualities of her Common Reader. These scholars tend to view

Woolf's Common Reader as an ideal, almost actual person whose behavior is described in Woolf's criticism. Constructions of the Common Reader have attached the concept to Woolf's political and social beliefs, and to her preoccupation with her role as a critic and scholar. The Common Reader, according to some critics, has become a persona adopted by Woolf to avoid the authoritarian stance she argues against. For example, Barbara Currier Bell and Carol Ohmann do not even acknowledge that the Common Reader is a figure borrowed from Johnson, wrought with eighteenth-century connotations. The Common Reader, according to these critics, is an invention that helps Woolf to address her audience:

> [Woolf] solves . . . the problem of how to address her readers amiably and unpretentiously, and her solution is crucial to her overall success as a critic. For she is not traditionally authoritarian, not an eminence, not a lecturer in her mode of relationship to her audience. Instead of a stance of omniscience . . . Woolf invents "the common reader" persona convincingly. (51)

Jean Guiguet takes the title "Common Reader" literally and, like Bell and Ohmann, sees it as Woolf's vehicle for dealing with an audience.

> Without prejudicing the justness of the epithet "common" or "average" with which she professes to make her reader represent a category broad enough to ensure her criticism a universality which would be its justification, we see from the start that Virginia Woolf is opposed to learned, academic criticism. (132)

For M. Manuel the issue is whether Woolf is "referring to herself in the title or to the class of readers for whom she is writing" (28). The "figure of the Common Reader as it emerges from the two series of essays is, like the Tiresias of Eliot's *Wasteland*, an indefinite and all inclusive figure. . . . The Common Reader is nothing but a mask that Virginia Woolf wore in her role as a critic" (29). Finally, Vijay L. Sharma sees Woolf's reliance on the Common Reader as "a measure of critical sanity which derives its force from a democratic bias, which may well have been grounded in her father's political faith" (19). To ignore the centrality of the Common Reader's point of view, according to Sharma, would be to miss the uniqueness of Woolf's critical position: "While most of her contemporaries were shoring up academic criticism . . . she was trying to bring the high-brow activity in line with the needs of the average reader" (89).

However, the Common Reader is more than an ideal reader or a persona that Woolf uses to address her audience: the Common Reader is a metaphor for how texts operate and how knowledge is constructed. With our understanding of the Common Reader as a rhetorical function rather than a persona used to address political and social agendas, we see how Woolf's title for her two collections of essays, *The Common Reader*, points to both its own textuality and the unifying theme of the books as a whole.[9] Not only does she describe how her reader reads, but her rhetoric mimics the very process she describes. Her rhetoric often contains literal dialogue, but it also has a number of points of view on a subject, and these points of view interact with each other as though in conversation. The Common Reader, whose function it is to trust experience rather than defer to authority, must engage in conversation to determine his or her point of view through contrast with another. The parallel between Woolf's Common Reader and her rhetoric is found in her concept of conversation and dialogue. The nonhierarchical quality of the Common Reader is merged with the concept of dialogue, while at the same time allowing the Common Reader to take on the other functions that dialogue implies.

Dialogue, as a model for constructing knowledge, is not fixed or static, but fluid, decentered, and process oriented. Like the Common Reader, dialogue is antiauthoritarian and nondidactic, unsystematic, and constantly changing with each interaction. Dialogue becomes part of Woolf's rhetoric, allowing opposing ideas to exist simultaneously and creating unity through contrariety in her "conversations" with herself. Johnson's influence on Woolf can be found not only in their shared idea of the reader, but in the importance they place on conversation.[10] Conversation as a rhetorical technique is the more penetrating and profound aspect of Johnson's writing that Woolf inherits, an element to which Stephen was unable to respond. Writing as conversation implies an interaction between the writer and reader, between the speaker and audience. The writer is also always a reader who is in dialogue with a precursor. The exchange in roles as reader and writer and the process of conversation between them are themselves fluid and never settle into a stagnant and unchanged position. In the essays Woolf makes much use of this relationship. What happens in her later work is an incorporation of this notion into the rhetoric of her prose: the writer's text is proleptic, anticipates its reception, and contains utterances to address that future reading.

We begin to see Woolf's application of conversation in oral and written communication as criteria for evaluating prose in her essay "Addison." Woolf assumes that her audience finds the content of Addison's essays not quite accessible. This is because "our standards have changed" and "a change of manners is often quite enough to put us out of touch altogether" (97).

Literature is written to engage its reader, since reading is a process of inter-action. We must read Addison as our contemporary and see what he has to offer us; we must "rub off such incrustations . . . and see what, for us in our time, remains" (99). What remains in Addison is "the not so despicable virtue . . . of being readable" (100).

What quality is it that makes Addison's prose so readable? We sense that the *Spectator* and *Tatler,* according to Woolf, are "nothing but talk" (99): Addison's readability lies in his conversational skills. She says, "[H]is essays at their very best preserve the very cadence of easy yet exquisitely modulated conversation. . . . [H]e seems to speak what comes into his head, and is never at the trouble of raising his voice" (102). Woolf's essay contains a passage describing Addison's conversational skills as they are exercised in the cof-feehouses. She tells us: "Here we have the Addison of Will's and Button's, who, sitting late into the night and drinking more than was good for him, gradually overcame his taciturnity and began to talk" (102). Woolf employs an image of Addison speaking to his auditors, allowing the analogy to his writing style to take on the characteristics of conversational interaction. This analogy has important implications and should be kept in mind when look-ing at Woolf's deployment of conversation in her other essays and novels.

Woolf defines Addison's style as one that makes "prose . . . prosaic" (105). He has developed a "medium which makes it possible for people of ordinary intelligence to communicate their ideas to the world" (105). For Woolf, conversation is the mode of the Common Reader because it allows one to acquire knowledge through an oral exchange. It is an easier, more fluid method of communication, where the response of one speaker is—if it is true conversation—the function of the response of another; this causes the content of the interaction to shift as each speaker talks. Addison's skill as converser in prose enables his readers to understand him and to talk back because the language of conversation appeals to the reader's common sense. As the reader's thoughts or voice echoes against Addison's, it becomes clear to the reader whether or not he or she agrees or disagrees. The elements that make prose prosaic are its similarities to conversation: the ease of commu-nication through an appeal to common sense and the speaking voice in dia-logue with other voices.

We may then understand that for Woolf it is the conversational aspect of prose that gives prose its openended, invitational quality. It is this aspect that Woolf investigates and develops throughout her growth as a writer, and it is this aspect that takes on a variety of forms: from the conversational frame she gives many of the essays to the use of dialogue in her essays and novels and the dialogical style found in the major novels. Woolf pursues her inquiry into the nature of conversation by analyzing the role of the reader or auditor in relation to the writer or speaker. Conversation for Woolf means not merely an oral exchange between two or more people, but ultimately the communication between different points of view, where one point of view is the function of every other point of view it comes into contact with. Conversation or dialogue is interactional and relational; Woolf's theory of language is based on this belief, and it informs her notions of reading and writing.

Woolf's experimentation with dialogue and conversation took place early in her career. But before we can understand the relationship between the Common Reader (the rhetorical figure rather than the person) and conversation (as a rhetorical strategy), we should see how these ideas have their origin in essays such as "Byron and Mr. Briggs" and "Mr. Conrad: A Conversation."

Woolf tried to articulate the method of the Common Reader in the essay "Byron and Mr. Briggs," an essay that was intended as the introduction to the proposed book *Reading* (referred to in the diary entry of May 23, 1921), which was never completed in the form suggested by the essay. As Andrew McNeillie points out, "[T]he ideas behind it were subsequently developed and recast until they evolved and emerged as *The Common Reader: First Series* (1925)" (473). [T]he ideas represented in "Byron and Mr. Briggs," such as the use of conversation to illustrate how the Common Reader communicates and understands the world and literature, are finally expressed in a prefatory essay to *The Common Reader* entitled "The Common Reader." How the Common Reader functions within Woolf's first collection of essays can be best understood with a reading of "Byron and Mr. Briggs."

The Mr. Briggs Woolf creates lived in the early nineteenth century, read Shakespeare, and resisted Coleridge's influence on his reading (480). The prototype of the Common Reader, Mr. Briggs has a certain kind of sense, a sense that Johnson defined and Woolf borrows. She tells us:

> When Johnson talked of the common sense of readers, no doubt he meant that the faculty of knowing what to use, what to neglect, is well developed among us, and can be trusted in the long run to whittle away even the enormous deposits which have heaped themselves over a man like Byron. (485)

How is it that the Common Reader develops this faculty of knowing, and what is the easiest way for the reader to exercise his knowledge? The answer seems to be through conversation. What follows Woolf's analysis of the common sense of readers is a scenario of a conversation. The scene verges on fiction, and the characters' voices and points of view become

Woolf's: "<Here is a little party of ordinary people, sitting round the dinner table, & talking, about Byron><gossiping; who will marry who; what the Prime Minister said, have you read Byron's letters>" (494). The conversants are Terence Hewett, Rose Shaw, Clarissa Dalloway, and Mr. Pepper, and through their conversation Woolf enacts the way in which the Common Reader comes to construct the meaning and knowledge of what he reads.

Rose Shaw and Terence Hewett enter the library. In describing the exchange between them, Woolf also includes what appears to be irrelevant and domestic information. Rose and Hewett discuss *Tristram Shandy* and, as Woolf tells us, so far as life and literature seem to help each other out, they "were using literature partly in order to make them understand each other" (495). It is through conversation that they get to know literature, and by knowing literature they get to know themselves. This is how the Common Reader operates— by making literature and reading part of life, and life part of literature and reading. Conversation therefore functions as a means of understanding and constructing interpretations, while it is through literature that we negotiate our way through social conversation.

This insight is pursued and developed by Woolf in "Mr. Conrad: A Conversation," written in 1923, the same year *The Common Reader* was being revised for publication. The essay also alludes to the problems of canon formation and literary history that Woolf will pursue in *A Room of One's Own*. The essay is a conversation between Penelope Otway, the ideal Common Reader, and her friend, David Lowe. We are told that Penelope Otway and her sisters, like Woolf, have access to their father's library and are allowed "to amuse themselves by reading what they liked" (76). Here the literal and metaphoric fathers give their female children access to the knowledge found in the library. Penelope is "content to read and to talk, reading at intervals of household business, and talking when she could find company" (76).

On the particular day Woolf describes, Penelope is visited by David Lowe, who finds her on the lawn surrounded by volumes of Joseph Conrad. Her conversation is held with a male auditor while the writer she discusses is one of the fathers of modern literature. Penelope sees Conrad as a classic writer, whereas Lowe does not—the conversation concentrates on this disagreement. Woolf will illustrate how literary value can be determined in a more feminine way—through the dialogic rhetoric of her text. Lowe finds fault because there is "nothing colloquial in Conrad; nothing intimate; and no humour, at least of the English kind" (77). Another fault is that Conrad is a romantic who has "never faced his disillusionment" (77). He "sings the same songs" and is "a mind of one fact" (78), and this kind of mind can never find a place among the classics.

Penelope counters Lowe by saying that Conrad is "not one and simple; no, he is many and complex" (78). Conrad is like many modern writers, including Woolf, who have multiple selves and whose texts function to realign themselves with each other. Woolf does not reject Conrad, but imitates and reflects him in yet another kind of dialogue. In the following passage Penelope expands on her theory of what constitutes a "classic." We can also see this passage as the essay's commentary on itself, the description of how and why conversation and dialogue function in a text, and, finally, how this passage notes what Woolf attempts to achieve in her own fiction. Penelope explains,

> And it is when they bring these selves into relation—when they simplify, when they reconcile their opposites—that they bring off . . . those complete books which for that reason we call their masterpieces. And Mr. Conrad's selves are particularly opposite. He is composed of two people who have nothing whatever in common. (79)

To create a great novel, an author must find some way to reconcile his conflicting selves. This essay demonstrates a method with which Woolf is experimenting: it is the use of conversation to allow "particularly opposite" points of view to come into relation with one another and to interact. The essay—and the problem of "greatness" that is its real subject—is not resolved; that is, Woolf as the author refuses to come down on either side of the debate. Instead, she has Penelope celebrate flux and movement as elements of literary value, thereby presenting an alternative to the authoritarian stance in criticism.

Lowe asks Penelope in which novel it is that Conrad achieves the unity of opposing selves. Penelope responds by saying she has just read Conrad's *Chance*, which she sees as "a great book." But, as she tells Lowe, "now you will have to read it yourself, for you are not going to accept my word, especially when it is a word I cannot define" (80). Penelope cannot "define" a "great" book for the same reason Johnson could not fix the meanings in his *Dictionary*; it is impossible to make a word or a book mean the same thing to all of its readers. Penelope, the Common Reader, is encouraging Lowe to become a Common Reader too. She acknowledges that she cannot and will not define and articulate her final judgment for someone else. Lowe must make his own decision based on his own experience. He must read the text and converse about and with it. She also illustrates the same process that Woolf has used in her reading of Samuel Johnson; Woolf has found techniques for narrative in her mentor's work and uses them, just as Penelope uses conversation, to move beyond him.

Conversation for the Common Reader is both the process of obtaining knowledge and the very goal of that process. Just as we know Conrad through the interaction of his opposing selves, so too do we know Woolf through opposing views in the essay—she is both Penelope and Lowe. Woolf refuses to tell her reader what to think about Conrad because she herself thinks many—often opposing—things. What Penelope tells Lowe, Woolf tells us: we must read Conrad for ourselves. Then, after we have read him, we must, again like Penelope, converse when we can—not to impose our views on others, but to clarify our thoughts, through contrast and opposition, for ourselves. Woolf encourages her readers to approach reading the same way, to use conversation, whether with texts or other readers, to clarify our thoughts and experience. By rooting criticism and evaluation in process, Woolf redefines the role of the critic.

Woolf begins to merge her preoccupation with conversation and the Common Reader in the structure of the collection entitled *The Common Reader.* Before she settled on the final structure of her first *Common Reader,* she had another idea for its organization. It would allow Woolf to debate herself, to avoid committing herself to a fixed opinion or judgment, to allow opposing views to exist simultaneously, and to become both the reader and the writer in a single act. On August 17, 1923 she writes in her diary:

> The question I want to debate here is the question of my essays, & how to make them into a book. The brilliant idea has just come to me of embedding them in Otway conversation. The main advantage would be that I could then comment, & add what I had to leave out, or failed to get in e.g. the one on George Eliot certainly needs an epilogue. Also to have a setting for each would "make a book"; & the collection of articles is in my view an inartistic method. But then this might be too artistic. . . . There could be an introductory chapter. A family which reads the papers. The thing to do wd. be to envelope each essay into its own atmosphere. To get them into a current of life, & so to shape the book.

Woolf was now considering framing *The Common Reader* in what she called "Otway conversation," the same method of experimentation in "Mr. Conrad." This frame, she felt, could allow her to say things that the structure of the traditional and "inartistic" book of articles could not. By constructing each of the essays in the form of a conversation between family members, she could place the essays into the "current of life" (a phrase taken from Johnson's *Rasselas*). The family would read the papers and then talk with each other about them, much in the same way as Rose and Terence did in "Byron and Mr. Briggs."

Conversation allows Woolf to interact with her own ideas, to agree and disagree with herself, and to allow her thinking about a text to be fluid without obligating herself to a view she knows might eventually change. She decided, however, not to pursue this idea out of fear it would take too much out of her: "[I]t might run away with me; it will take time." Here we find Woolf's awareness of the dangers of conversation. Her active mind and constant rethinking and reworking of ideas in her writing make her acutely aware of the nature of conversation in written discourse. Her ability to converse with herself, while it gave her one of her greatest critical insights, was her most troublesome and devastating skill because of her knowledge that the conversational mode does not have closure and resolution.

In her lifetime, Woolf collected and organized two series of essays, both entitled *The Common Reader*. The two collections contain a number of essays that have as their subject the process of reading and writing, and the relation between the reader and writer. Her preface to the first collection, entitled "The Common Reader," defines the Common Reader, as did Johnson, as one who "differs from the critic and scholar" (1). He is "guided by an instinct to create for himself, out of whatever odds and ends he can come by, some kind of whole" (1). By beginning with this essay, Woolf establishes the organization of the collection. But are we to believe that what is to follow is just "a few ideas and opinions" that are "insignificant in themselves" (2)? It is not the humbleness of her endeavor that Woolf wishes to emphasize, but the process of construction and the lack of a fixed position. What the Common Reader does—his purpose, motivation, and strategies—is the same as the writer; they both share an "instinct to create . . . some kind of whole." Reading is writing, and writing is reading: both are acts of interpretation and the construction of knowledge. And it is the acts of interpretation and construction that are the unifying themes of the collection.

By beginning the collection with her essay on the Common Reader, she achieves a similar end to that of "Otway conversation." The essays are the expressions of a Common Reader, the creations and constructions of a mind in dialogue with a text. The essays do not contain the authority of the scholar or critic, but rather the opinions and perceptions of readers at a certain moment who, with their next reading experience or conversation, will create new meaning. The reader's mind is fluid, not static, and the essays in *The Common Reader* represent this constant flux and interaction, for they suggest a mind in conversation.

The reader's role in determining the meaning of a text is found in "The Patron and the Crocus," where how and what an author writes are functions of something outside the author, not the product of one's isolated imagina-

tion. Woolf will later develop this notion in her unfinished work, "Anon."
There she explains the relationship between author, audience, and influence:

> The poet is . . . attached to his audience. tethered [sic] to one spot
> and played upon by outside influences. Some are visible to himself
> only; others show themselves only when time has past. As the
> book goes out into a larger, a more varied audience these influences
> become more and more complex. (390)

"The Patron and the Crocus" is also reminiscent of Johnson's *Adventurer* No.
85, where he points out the inability of the isolated mind to counter arguments it has never considered. We find Woolf defining both the writing and
the reading processes as interactional. There can be no writing without
something prior to initiate its movement: "For a book is always written for
somebody to read, and, since the patron is not merely the paymaster, but
also in a very subtle and insidious way the instigator and inspirer of what
is written, it is of the utmost importance that he should be a desirable man"
(206). The patron is a kind of audience, but an audience that differs from
the reader. He is the prior utterance, the statement said before the writer
talks, the father and origin of what is spoken by beginning conversation.
    It is not so much that content is determined by the patron; rather, the
patron determines how the author writes and the way his ideas are
expressed. So that the writer "who has been moved by the sight of the first
crocus in Kensington Gardens has, before he sets pen to paper, to choose
from a crowd of competitors the particular patron who suits him best"
(207). The patron is not a predetermined father, but is chosen by the writer,
just as Woolf has chosen Johnson. The writer knows the importance of his
choice because he is picking his own beginning, as arbitrary and artificial
as that beginning might be. Writing, according to Woolf, is "a method of
communication; and the crocus is an imperfect crocus until it has been
shared" (207). And this communication occurs not only between the writer
and the reader, but between the writer and his patron.
    When looking for a patron, the one we want is the one who will "help us
to preserve our flowers from decay" (208). But who will be the appropriate patron is the difficult thing to gauge. The qualities of the correct audience "change from age to age," as Woolf notes in her essay on Addison, "and
it needs considerable integrity and conviction not to be dazzled by the pre-
tensions or bamboozled by the persuasions of the competing crowd, this
business of patron-finding is one of the tests and trials of authorship" (208).
For Woolf, to know "whom to write for is to know how to write" (208). The
patron and the writer are symbiotically connected, and the patron must

"efface himself or assert himself as his writers require; that he is bound to them by a more than material tie; that they are twins indeed, one dying if the other dies, one flourishing if the other flourishes; that the fact of literature depends upon their happy alliance" (210) cannot be denied. The writer cannot exist without an audience, and though the audience may be varied and diverse, it is important that the writer choose the right patron.

And so we find that for Woolf the idea that a writer is not only speaking to someone else, but *because* of someone else, is crucial, and it helps us to understand her emphasis on the notions of conversation and voice in writing. The readers must hear the author's voice so that they can respond to it and enter into conversation with it, for the readers' responses are as dependent on the author's voice as the author is dependent on his audience. Woolf will pursue this vital relationship in *Between the Acts*. Not only does the audience determine what is being said, but how it is said, and it is the influence of the audience on the style of the essay that Woolf addresses in "The Modern Essay."

In describing what the modern essay entails, Woolf notes that the shape and the nature of the essay shift through history, from the time of Addison to the present, and the shape of the essay is a function of its audience. The Victorian essayists (and Woolf's father is a clear example) had something in common: "They wrote at greater length than is now usual, and they wrote for a public which had not only time to sit down to its magazine seriously, but a high, if peculiarly Victorian, standard of culture by which to judge it" (215). But during Woolf's time the audience had changed, and so too the essayist and essay. "But a change from a small audience of cultivated people to a larger audience of people who were not so cultivated" leads us to a "common reader," and is perhaps a "reversion to the classic type, and that the essay losing its size and something of its sonority was approaching the essay of Addison and Lamb" (211). The essay is still alive and as conditions change, "so the essayist . . . adapts himself, and if he is good makes the best of the change, and if he is bad the worst" (216).

Of those essayists who have adapted themselves to the audience of their time, Max Beerbohm, for Woolf, is one of the best. Beerbohm's audience demanded that the essayist give "himself," something which, Woolf claims, "had been in exile since the death of Charles Lamb" (216). Beerbohm's essays "must have surprised readers accustomed to exhortation, information, and denunciation to find themselves familiarly addressed by a voice which seemed to belong to a man no larger than themselves" (217). Mr. Beerbohm brought "personality into literature . . . consciously and purely." We are told that the "spirit of personality permeates every word he writes" (217).

And this is his "triumph of style" (217). When we read Beerbohm's essays we feel that "we shall sit down with them and talk" (218).

In criticizing Belloc's essays, Woolf says that the personality of his essays suffer because it "comes to us not with the natural richness of speaking voice" but like "the voice of a man shouting through a crowd on a windy day" (218-19). The contemporary audience consists of "busy people catching trains in the morning" and "tired people coming home in the evening," and it is a "kind, tired, apathetic world for which [essayists] write" (219-20). This is what forces the essay writer to write in a concentrated and concise manner, but, paradoxically, "the shrinkage in size [of the essay] has brought a corresponding expansion of individuality" (220). We no longer have the "'I' of Max and Lamb, but the 'we' of public bodies and other sublime personages" (220).

Therefore, we see the importance of a speaking voice in Woolf's assessment of the essay. The quality of the voice is crucial; the contemporary audience demands that the essayist be able to engage it in tone as well as content—the "how" as well as the "what" of the essay. No matter who the audience, the awareness of audience is crucial, for the "art of writing has for backbone some fierce attachment to an idea" and the audience forces "something believed in with conviction or seen with precision and thus compelling words to its shape" (221).

In "How it Strikes a Contemporary," the final essay in her first *Common Reader,* Woolf reiterates the role of the reader's response in determining the value of classical and contemporary writing. Johnson's critical precepts, which we saw articulated in his expectations of the Common Reader, are again found in Woolf's expression of the relationship between the critic and the reader. Though *The Common Reader* is arranged chronologically, with such essays as "The Pastons and Chaucer," "Notes on an Elizabethan Play," "Defoe," and "George Eliot," "How it Strikes a Contemporary" focuses on the process of evaluation rather than its subject. It can be read as a companion piece to the essay "The Common Reader," as a map for understanding and constructing the essays that precede it. The method for doing so is the same as the method Woolf delineates in "Hours in a Library": determining value is a constructed and deferred process. The value of the past is determined only through the present, and the present is determined in relation to the future.

The problem arises when we know that two critics "at the same table at the same moment will pronounce completely different opinions about the same book" (231). The only advice that the two critics could possibly offer is that the reader should "respect one's own instincts, to follow them fearlessly and, rather than submit them to the control of any critic or reviewer alive, to check them by reading and reading over again the masterpieces of the past" (232). Like Penelope Otway, who taught the reader to enter into dialogue to understand his or her own thoughts, Woolf's critic offers the reader the encouragement to trust common sense and to develop that common sense through extensive reading.

Woolf realizes that there is no way to gauge a masterpiece during the present time. She recommends "that it would be wise for the writers of the present to renounce the hope of creating masterpieces" (240). Instead, writers should look at their work as poised in the middle of the process, just as the writer himself is, never knowing its value until value is constructed by the future. For Woolf, it is "from the notebooks of the present that the masterpieces of the future are made" (240). The role of the critic, then, is shifted— it is not a position from which to give a value judgement. A critic should comment on process—the process of the writer and the reader, and the process by which masterpieces are determined. Woolf calls on critics to be "generous of encouragement," to take "a wider, less personal view of modern literature, and look indeed upon the writers as if they were engaged upon some vast building, which being built by common effort, the separate workmen may well remain anonymous" (240). We can only "see the past," not in relation to the present, but "in relation to the future; and so prepare the way for masterpieces to come" (241). The critical endeavor is one of seeing connections, of understanding the past in relation to the fleeting present and the present in terms of the unknown future. The critics themselves do not know if their judgments will stand the test of time; they can only compare and view things in relation to each other, just as Johnson did in his Preface to *Shakespeare*. The crucial difference between the reader and the critic is that the critic has read so much, has such a great repertoire and basis for comparison, that he or she can more confidently (though not necessarily correctly) make decisions.

Woolf also addresses these issues in "How Should One Read a Book?" (1932), an essay that concludes her second series of *The Common Reader*. In this essay Woolf tells us how to read her; she reminds us, as Common Readers, to take responsibility for our reading. The beginning of this essay echoes her preface to the first series and reminds us of Johnson's famous declaration:

> To admit authorities, however heavily furred and gowned into our libraries and let them tell us how to read, what to read, what value to place upon what we read, is to destroy the spirit of freedom which is the breath of those sanctuaries. Everywhere else we have been bound by laws and conventions—there we have none. (234)

As a critic herself, Woolf describes critics as merely more experienced readers; and readers can become critics, not by following critical rules or laws, but by reading and comparing through dialogue. Woolf admonishes us to read on our own, to be the Common Reader, and to learn to judge literature according to our own experience. There are no proscribed ways to read and write, no "laws and conventions," no authorities to threaten us.

Again, she conflates the reading and writing processes: "Perhaps the quickest way to understand the elements of what a novelist is doing is not to read, but to write; to make your own experiment with the dangers and difficulties of words" (235). Here we find another important dialogic configuration: reading and writing are processes that can only be understood in relation to one another; they are in many ways one and the same. Reading is a process that helps us to "exercise our own creative powers" (239), a creativity with which we are familiar in our writing and which is often seen as the outlet for our imagination.

There is a method to the reading process, a way of putting shape and form to the impressions we receive. To "receive impressions with the utmost understanding" is only the first part of the process, but it "must be completed, if we are to get the whole pleasure from a book" (241). And the second part of the process, "to judge, to compare" (242), is by no means as simple as the first. The second part of the process is one of comparing, of judging the value of one book by contrasting it with another. This means, of course, that to judge one reading experience one must have many reading experiences, and that the comparison of one book with another in the reader's mind creates a conversation between works. It is this conversation that illuminates meaning: "To continue reading without the book before you, to hold one shadow-shape against another, to have read widely enough and with enough understanding to make such comparisons alive and illuminating—that is difficult" (243).

Critics are people who have read so much that there is a dialogue between works occurring in their thought processes while they read—and this is what makes them critics. And this, I argue, is exactly what Woolf, Stephen, and Johnson do when they read and write. It is the connections within their writing and reading processes that we, as readers and critics of their work, must try to articulate. To carry out the second part of the reader's duty needs "such imagination, insight, and learning that it is hard to conceive any one mind sufficiently endowed" (243). A critic has read widely and does not tell us what to read, but illuminates texts that we have already read and answers questions that we have already formed.

> Coleridge and Dryden and Johnson, in their considered criticism
> . . . are surprisingly relevant; they light up and solidify the vague
> ideas that have been tumbling in the misty depths of our minds.
> But they are only able to help us if we come to them laden with
> questions and suggestions won honestly in the course of our read-
> ing. . . . We can only understand their ruling when it comes in con-
> flict with our own. (244)

We learn from critics only when their judgments "conflict" or differ from our
own. This is the function of criticism—to create a sense of difference so that
we may understand our own thoughts, thoughts that find their meaning
through contrast, dialogue, or conversation with other thoughts. Criticism
is not a meaning or interpretation constructed in the isolated and singular
reading experience of some better equipped sensibility that teaches us the
correct vision of the world. Criticism engages us in conversation, and the
critic calls attention to the process of conversation or dialogue so that he and
his fellow Common Readers can clarify their thoughts through the reading
process. These Common Readers are the ones with which Johnson and
Woolf rejoice.

The use of conversation and the setting up of oppositions to create some
kind of unity or whole are found in various forms of Woolf's review essays,
the essays *A Room of One's Own* and *Three Guineas*, and her major fiction from
Mrs. Dalloway through *Between the Acts*. As a member of the Bloomsbury
group, she made conversation an important part of her life, an activity that
helped her sort out her ideas and perceptions as well as the thinking of her
companions. It is not unusual, then, that when she came upon Johnson's
emphasis on conversation as a metaphor for good writing, she should
expand and develop it into a prose technique that places her among the best
twentieth-century experimental writers.

CHAPTER

♦4♦

Dialogue and Subjectivity:
A Room of One's Own, Mrs. Dalloway,
and *To the Lighthouse*

Samuel Johnson's influence on Virginia Woolf is found in the way he shaped both her reading process and her understanding of how knowledge and meaning are created. For Woolf and Johnson, knowledge and meaning are found not only in our interactions with texts, but in the dialogue within ourselves and with the world outside of ourselves. There is no voice, origin, or place where meaning rests securely. When Johnson writes in *The Rambler* of the need for the writer to interact with the world, to participate in the "interchange of thoughts which is practised in free and easy conversation" (IV: 108), he points to the process of identity formation itself. Knowledge, of the self or the world, must always be acquired through an "interchange" between points of view. The Common Reader, as Woolf and Johnson begin to understand it, is a locus for those points of view. Its participation in dialogue is the very process that creates its identity and meaning.

Woolf discovered the value and significance of dialogue in her critical essays, both as a way of articulating the content of those essays, as well as a method for organizing them. We know that Woolf was satisfied with neither the form of critical prose nor that of fictional narrative. The greatest problem for Woolf as a writer was the split she found in her own thinking; there are the "critical" and the "creative," which are, on the one hand, vehemently opposed, and on the other, somehow inextricably linked. Throughout *A Writer's Diary* we find her struggling with the question of form.

Roger Poole argues that the conflict Woolf experienced was the product of her being surrounded by thinkers—her father and Leonard Woolf—whose rationalist tendencies were antithetical to her model of thinking and writing (Poole 20), a model of thinking which I've termed dialogic. Woolf describes her depression with the same vocabulary as she talks of her writing: "I tried to analyze my depression: how my brain is jaded with the conflict within of two types of thought, the critical, the creative; how I am harassed by the strife and jar and uncertainty without" (May 26, 1932). For Woolf, the creative and the critical are related to her sense of inner and outer worlds; for her these terms represent opposition and difference. Her desire was to find an artistic form that would embrace both modes of thought: "And what is my own position towards the inner and the outer? I think a kind of ease and dash are good;—yes: I think even externality is good; some combination of them ought to be possible" (November 28, 1928). So, at moments we find Woolf stating, "I want to write criticism" (December 8, 1929), because it "absorbs me more and more" (February 18, 1922). And at other moments, she feels oppressed by critical thought: "After a dose of criticism I feel that I'm writing sideways, using only an angle of my mind. This is justification; for free use of the faculties means happiness" (June 13, 1923). As an artist, her project was to develop literary and critical genres that helped her to express her particular vision of reality. She sought forms that would reconcile the conflicts that bring on depression. The critical and creative could never be fully synthesized, so she developed forms that could contain the two antithetical modes of thought. These forms evolved into complicated narrative strategies that incorporate the dialogic qualities she inherited from Samuel Johnson and defined in her early critical essays. Each narrative strategy evokes the process of construction that she argued the Common Reader utilizes and represents.

The Common Reader, as Woolf defines it, is a metaphor for narrative construction itself, for the Common Reader molds his or her experience and meaning through a dialogic interaction with the world, whether that interaction is through literal conversation or through the written texts of other readers. The Common Reader is a vehicle for Woolf to discuss subjectivity detached from personality, to show how identity interacts with and is affected by the world around it. The Common Reader, in other words, is an interpreter, and Woolf's goal is to demonstrate the various ways meaning is constructed. Through dialogue the Common Reader does not unearth or reveal the meaning but creates it; this meaning can never be finalized and is, therefore, subject to perpetual discussion.

The Common Reader helps to define the communication that occurs between a reader and a writer as one that is gained through active understanding.[1] In active understanding the listener is not only concerned with what is being said, but with why it is being said; he relates it to his own interests and assumptions, imagines how the utterance responds to future utterances, evaluates it, and intuits how third parties will understand it. The listener must also go through a process of preparing a response.[2] The narrative strategies of Woolf's novels *Mrs. Dalloway* (1925) and *To the Lighthouse* (1927), and her longer critical treatise, *A Room of One's Own* (1929), illustrate her experimentation and development of various modes of dialogic subjectivity and enact the process of understanding that occurs between a Common Reader and the world.[3]

Woolf investigates the relation between inner and outer worlds by creating a narrative that questions the construction of the speaking subject.[4] It is through an investigation of the speaking subject that Woolf questions the nature of subjectivity. The construction of identity and subjectivity through the interaction of points of view both within and outside of the subject is pursued by Woolf in *A Room of One's Own*. *A Room* problematizes its own authority through the subjectivity of the speaker, and it is also an experiment in narrative voice and subject, used to portray an alternative history. In this essay it is not the subjectivity of a specific character that Woolf uses as a vehicle, but in a bolder and more experimental manner, it is the subjectivity of the narrator herself. The essay as a genre is assumed to address the world within which the author is writing; that is, the writing voice belongs to the author, not to a constructed persona. However, Woolf does not allow us to identify the "I" of the essay with her, and so we are forced to consider how the authority of the narrative is established, if it is at all. In *A Room* we find Woolf breaking down the genres of fiction and critical prose as she tries to find a way to incorporate her own conflicting modes of thought. The first thing Woolf does is to fictionalize the speaker, much in the same way Johnson does in his *Rambler, Idler,* and *Adventurer* essays. By fictionalizing the speaker the authors remove their own personalities from the points of view they are espousing. The sense of security the reader gains from knowing the author, as a being in the real world, grounded in real experience, is lost. The reader is forced to call on experience when reading the essays. The authority of the essay, which was once found in the author, is now found in the reader, who constructs meaning as he or she moves through the text.

Early in the essay Woolf signals the problem of narrative authority:

> I need not say that what I am about to describe has no existence;
> Oxbridge is an invention; so is Fernham; "I" is only a convenient
> term for somebody who has no real being. Lies will flow from my
> lips, but there may perhaps be some truth mixed with them; it is
> for you to seek out this truth and to decide whether any part of it
> is worth keeping. (4)

The essay form, by convention, implies that its discourse contains, reflects,
or transcribes the reality it discusses, and that the writing voice is Woolf's.
That is, the language of the essay is more denotative than connotative; it is
more fact than fiction. However, what Woolf describes is a history of women
that does not exist, and she does so by assuming many voices and points of
view. And, though her audience is a group of women, her argument is
directed against a masculine institutional perspective. By problematizing the
first person "I" it is unclear who is speaking and to whom, whether the perspective that the "I" represents is fiction or fact, objective or subjective. It
is ironic that Woolf uses the fictional narrative of the essay and the dialogized subject she inherits from Johnson to discuss the lack of a female literary canon. However, it is Woolf's articulation of this lack, based on
methods she read in Johnson, that begins the series of voices and conversations that will create the tradition she calls for.

The speaker of the essay knows how difficult, if not impossible, it is to
give the audience "a nugget of pure truth" (3). She claims she will offer an
"opinion" and "develop in your presence as fully and freely as I can the train
of thought which led me to think this" (4). What we will get is not the
"truth" about women and fiction, but a reflection on how an opinion came
to be constructed—its process and development. She will give the audience
the opportunity to draw its own conclusions by letting it observe "the limitations, the prejudices, the idiosyncrasies of the speaker" (4). At the end of
the essay she reflects and evaluates what she has written: "But when I look
back through these notes and criticize my own train of thought as I made
them, I find that my motives were not altogether selfish" (113). There is a
self-conscious artificiality about the rhetoric, where the speaking "I" knows
that everything she is and says is a construction.

To replicate the process through which she came to her conclusions, the
speaker takes on the points of view of three characters—Mary Beton, Mary
Seton, and Mary Carmichael—and she invites us to call her by any of those
names. It is "not a matter of any importance" (5) what we call her, for she is
all of them and none of them. Her one voice is the product of all their voices,

her opinion the evolution of all their opinions. The opinion that the speaker holds of women and fiction, besides that of women needing five hundred pounds a year and a room of their own, is that the female writer and female identity are made up of all the experiences of women before her, and determined by the women who follow. This, of course, is what is actually missing for Woolf as a writer. But she creates the tradition, through a fictionalization of women writers, in order to ground the meaning of the essay. Again, Woolf's own literary tradition, as we know, was not a purely female tradition, and it was a function of her literary dialogues with Johnson and Stephen, among others. It is the dialogues with these writers, her understanding and knowledge of their work, that gave her the tools to create the narrative of a feminist tradition. Woolf's essay reflects the multiplicity of perspectives and experience that she argues women must maintain. To understand the subjectivity of the "I" in the essay, we must look at the three women with whom she identifies.

The process by which the speaking "I" comes to her opinion on the multiplicity of identity begins with the passage concerning Mary Seton. The speaker begins by having a conversation with Mary Seton, using Mary as an auditor for her thoughts and feelings of the day's experiences; the speaker is both Mary Seton and someone other than Mary Seton. Everything Mary says and thinks is part of the speaker's point of view, and it is only through Mary's perspective that the experience of the men's colleges can be understood. After Mary tells how it took her and other women much time and effort to pull together thirty thousand pounds, the speaker begins to conjecture how and why it is that Mary's mother did not have the capital to help the school establish itself as the men's colleges had. It is, according to the speaker, a matter of history and tradition, and tradition dictates that women bear children and do not go into business.

If Mary's mother had gone into business, had become a "manufacturer of artificial silk or a magnate on the Stock Exchange," then she could have left the school two or three thousand pounds, and Mary and the speaker could discuss "archaeology, botany, anthropology, physics, the nature of the atom, mathematics, astronomy, relativity, geography" (21). However, if Mary's mother had gone into business there would be no Mary, and there would be no voice of the speaker, nor would there be the essay she is creating.

The speaker brings up all the possible issues that could effect the women's college while both talking to her reader and Mary Seton. Her words, thoughts, and arguments are determined by the same forces that have determined the history of Mary's college. It is because women have not gone into business, earned money, and owned property that the speaker is talking to the group about women and fiction.

The next persona or point of view that the speaker takes on is that of Mary Beton. In this passage, the speaker talks about what she can get from society, "chicken and coffee, bed and lodging," in return for pieces of paper left by her aunt, "for no other reason than that I share her name" (37). Mary Beton and the speaker are one and the same, and the perspective that Mary Beton brings, like Mary Seton's, is of the relationship between money and knowledge. The difference is that Beton's perspective shows how money can, in fact, effect perspective. The speaker's tone is not frustrated nor ironic as it was when she was at Fernham, but it is full of wonder at the power her purse can yield. Her aunt represents the rubbing away of the "rust and corrosion" and "the fear and bitterness" that accumulate through her experience with society. She finds herself adopting a new attitude toward "the other half of the human race": "It was absurd to blame any class or any sex, as a whole. Great bodies of people are never responsible for what they do" (38). The money that was left to Mary Beton allowed "fear and bitterness [to modify] themselves into pity and toleration" (39) and soon "pity and toleration went, and the greatest release of all came, which is the freedom to think of things in themselves" (39). With the release of fear and bitterness the mind is free to think about the world without coloring it with emotions. Her aunt's legacy "unveiled the sky" (39) to her. Through Mary Beton, the narrator can enter and describe the psychological process involved when a woman has access to money.

The third name that the speaker goes by is Mary Carmichael who, like Woolf, is a writer. Carmichael's perspective differs from Mary Seton, who testifies to women's lack of resources, and Mary Beton, who represents the acquisition of resources. Carmichael shows what one can do and achieve with the tradition and history of female power behind her. Carmichael is the "descendant of all those other women whose circumstances" the speaker has been glancing at (84). She represents the woman writer free of prejudice and anger, and her work represents the potential of writers to come. The speaker talks of reading Carmichael, a writer who, for the first time in the speaker's experience, writes from the female perspective. "Chloe liked Olivia" is a new line found in literature, and the speaker uses this opportunity to discuss why it hasn't been written yet, and what it will take to develop the line further. In actuality, this line was written by Woolf, not the fictional Carmichael, and it creates the initial statement necessary for a dialogue between women to begin. Fiction becomes the basis for history.

Woolf uses the speaker, the "I" of the narrative, to address issues that she has confronted as a woman writer. At the same time, the "I" is not Woolf, but is, as we have found, a combination of various personas presented in the essay. The subjective construction of the speaking "I" is developed through Mary Carmichael as the "I" challenges Carmichael's motives and techniques. The speaker both is and is not Mary Carmichael, and to know one identity we must know the other—there is conflict and interaction between the two personas. In a sense, the speaker is talking to herself about herself as she comments on Carmichael. In the same way, Woolf is talking about herself as she represents the dialogic subjectivity of the speaker through its interaction with the various characters described. She is pointing to the need of both Carmichael and herself to have a series of voices on which to base their own.

What Mary Carmichael is trying to achieve is new, and the speaker knows that if "Chloe likes Olivia and Mary Carmichael knows how to express it she will light a torch in the vast chamber where nobody has yet been" (88). When the speaker describes what will be needed, she shifts from third person to second, thereby speaking both to the audience and to herself. The speaker is aware of the artificiality of her address to Carmichael:

> The only way for you to do it, I thought, addressing Mary Carmichael as if she were there, would be to talk of something else, ... and thus note ... what happens when Olivia ... feels the light fall on [the window], and sees coming her way a piece of strange food—knowledge, adventure, art. (88-89)

In this passage Woolf comments on the strategy of her essay through the speaker. She knows that she is, like Carmichael and the speaking "I," bringing light to a vast chamber of experience that has not been articulated before. What Woolf does is "talk of something else"—Mary Carmichael, Mary Beton, and Mary Seton—in order to discuss how women will react to knowledge, adventure, and art. The rhetoric of the essay enacts Woolf's thesis on women and literature: there is no literary history for female writers, and what is needed is a tradition that can give women the dialogue of voices needed to construct their own voices. Women need a chamber of literary voices that their writing can echo and incorporate. Without this chamber, the voice of the woman writer might turn inwards, with no communication or dialogue with the world. Just as Woolf's tradition is one that echoes and incorporates the voices of Stephen and Johnson, women writers, according to Woolf, need one that consists only of women. For Woolf a purely female literary history will bring a diversity of voices into the dialogue of women writers. It is this awareness that makes Woolf one of the strongest advocates of feminism and women's writing. However, it is also highly ironic that the concepts and methods used to construct this ideal history are borrowed from her literary fathers.

This notion of a literary history for women is another thing we find in the speaker's portrayal of Mary Carmichael. The other purpose of Carmichael's writing is to record the lives of women that have never been recorded. We hear Woolf setting out her own path as a writer of history.[5]

> All these infinitely obscure lives remain to be recorded, I said, addressing Mary Carmichael as if she were present; and went on in thought through the streets of London feeling in imagination the pressure of dumbness, the accumulation of unrecorded life. (93)

Woolf had projected writing a history of unknown or minor personages: "I want to read voraciously and gather material for the *Lives of the Obscure* — which is to tell the whole history of England in one obscure life after another" (July 20, 1925). Woolf's *Lives* are in stark contrast to Johnson's *Lives of the Poets*. Where his histories are of the existing writers of his time, where he discusses their merits and faults, Woolf's *Lives* are histories of those who don't have histories. She feels the "pressure" of the silence and the "accumulation" of missing narrative. Hers is a projected history of lack, of the missing and unaccounted for, where value has no resonance because there is nothing to base it on.

The self-aware speaker not only allows her reader to know what she is thinking by her dialogue with Mary Carmichael, but in her voice we find voices composed of voices: there is Woolf who uses the voice of the "I"; the speaking "I" defines her voice as those of Mary Beton, Mary Seton, and Mary Carmichael; Mary Carmichael's voice is given articulation through the voices of the women writers who come before her; and, finally, so too is Woolf's voice composed of the women and writers discussed in the essay.

The interconnected nature of point of view and voice is Woolf's final statement on women and fiction, and it is with this issue that she closes the essay. The identification of all the personae in the essay with Mary Carmichael begins with an allusion to the experience at the beginning of the essay. The speaker hopes that Mary Carmichael "did not see, the bishops and the deans, the doctors and the professors, the patriarchs and the pedagogues all at her shouting warning and advice. . . . Fellows and scholars only allowed on the grass! Ladies not admitted without a letter of introduction!" (97). The speaker's experience is Carmichael's, and Carmichael's experience is ultimately Woolf's. There is something inhibiting about the masculine voice, the texts of her literary ancestors, and the most she can do is wish that the writers who follow will not experience the same sense of censorship that she has.

The essay ends with the illusion of shift in the speaking voice. We are told that "Here, then, Mary Beton ceases to speak" (109), and that "I will end now in my own person by anticipating two criticisms, so obvious that you can hardly fail to make them" (109). Who is the "I" who tells us this? If it is not Mary Beton, is it Mary Seton or Mary Carmichael? Is it some other persona created by Woolf to speak to us? Or is it Woolf herself? It is impossible to tell and it hardly matters. For at this juncture we come to realize that each individual voice is composed of all the other voices, and it is with this concept that the "I" addresses the issues of women, literature, and the history of women and literature.

The "I" tells us that "books have a way of influencing each other" (113). If we look at a great woman writer like Sappho or Emily Brontë we find that "she is an inheritor as well as an originator" (113). It is with this sense of tradition and history that we come to understand women and literature, and we begin to help Shakespeare's sister to develop her potential. For we draw her life "from the lives of the unknown who were her forerunners, as her brother did before her" (118). We cannot expect her to be born again to live and write "without that preparation, with that effort on our part, without that determination" (118). She will come "if we worked for her, and that so to work, even in poverty and obscurity, is worth while" (118). With this essay, Woolf justifies the life and work of her listeners and readers. No matter how obscure and insignificant they may be, their lives are linked to those women who came before them and to those who come after. The issue of women and literature is the issue of women and economics, politics, and the establishment of professions. Subjectivity, identity, and meaning are constructed by the world with which one interacts, as Woolf learned from Johnson, and it is in *A Room* that Woolf discovers the means to merge her political and psychological concerns by showing subjectivity as consisting of the subjectivities of the women she talks about.

Like *A Room of One's Own, Mrs. Dalloway* is a novel about subjectivity and how the subjective self interacts with, and is formed by, the world around it. And, again like *A Room*, critics have described the way the social and the public worlds are reflected in the content and theme of the novel rather than concentrating on the way the novel enacts the process by which inner and outer worlds become intertwined.[6] Johnson's emphasis on the social construction of meaning, and Woolf's search for a synthesis between the critical and creative, can be found in the narrative structure of this novel. In *Mrs. Dalloway* it is only through the social world that the protagonist can construct an understanding of who she is.

The issue of the subjective or psychological self is anticipated by Woolf in her essay "Modern Fiction." There she states that "the problem before the novelist at present . . . is to contrive means of being free to set down what he chooses," and the point of interest for him "lies very likely in the dark places of psychology." The emphasis on the internal workings of character, rather than the "materialist" detail of the external world, according to Woolf, have been ignored, and "at once a different outline of form becomes necessary, difficult for us to grasp, incomprehensible to our predecessors" (152). The signature of the modern British novel has been its ability to represent psychological reality. Early studies of the novel attempt to name and describe what has become known as the stream-of-consciousness technique, a technique that reflects the subjective element in modern narrative. The inability of critics to pinpoint exactly what the stream-of-consciousness technique is, and how it is achieved, illustrates the problematic nature of the concept.[7]

The concept of the stream-of-consciousness novel put forth by Melvin Friedman, Robert Humphrey, and Leon Edel, among others, assumes that the psyche is composed of a unified center of consciousness that is defined by its lack of rational logic and syntax. These authors argue that the lack of logic is represented in Woolf's (as well as other stream-of-consciousness writers) narrative strategies of free association and the juxtaposition of "subjective" points of view. With these contemporary theories of the subject, primarily Lacan's revision of the Freudian notion of the ego, Woolf's contribution to the novel can be reevaluated.[8] None of the studies on stream of consciousness consider that the subject being represented may in some way be split, composed of voices that come from *outside* the subject. There can be no place from which the psyche originates, nor is there any kind of subjectivity per se: there is only the *relation* between inner and outer worlds. What is occurring in Woolf's language is not free association but a simultaneity of spoken (or written) words and their meanings.

Through the characters Septimus Smith, Elizabeth Dalloway, and Clarissa Dalloway, Woolf delineates three paradigms of subjectivity with which we are to understand the novel. Johnson's emphasis on the necessity of the writer to enter into converse with the world rather than remain in isolation parallels Woolf's analysis of the subjective self. In a sense, individuals, like writers, create or write their own identity through an interaction with, and interpretation of, the world. Septimus, Elizabeth, and Clarissa are writers who read the signs and symbols of the world, while they are at the same time read by the world around them. The first paradigm we find in Septimus, whose subjectivity is projected onto the world though he is unable to connect or communicate with it; the second is represented by Elizabeth, Clarissa's daughter, whose identity is determined by those who perceive her, though we have little sense of how *she* perceives the world. The third mode of subjectivity, represented by Clarissa, is dialogical, where points of view interact simultaneously from within and outside of the subject.

Septimus Smith represents the mode of subjectivity in which points of view emanate from the subject. Septimus hears multiple voices and perspectives, but because all of these points of view are part of his own subjectivity, he can make no meaning out of them. Signs and symbols have for Septimus a floating signification—though he knows they mean something, he cannot determine what that meaning is. In two particular instances we find Septimus associated with symbols that have, literally, floating signification. The first is when we are introduced to Septimus, as he and others watch the airplane and try to decipher its writing. The letters that the airplane creates are a "thick ruffled bar of white smoke which curled and wreathed upon the sky" (29). The letters are undecipherable, for they are in constant movement: "But what letters? A C was it? and E, than an L?" (29). For only a moment do the letters lie still and then "they moved and melted and were rubbed up in the sky" (29). None of the readers can decode its meaning; Mrs. Coates thinks it reads "Glaxo" while Mrs. Bletchly reads "Kreemo." The clouds to which the letters attached themselves "moved freely" (30).

Septimus, unlike the others, knows that the clouds mean nothing, and though he thinks "they are signalling me" (31), he acknowledges that it is not "indeed in actual words; that is, he could not read the language yet; but it was plain enough, this beauty" (31). His wife, Lucrezia, wants to bring Septimus away from his mode of subjectivity, to get him to ascribe to the alternative notion of meaning. She wants him to have a point of view on an object outside himself. "Look," she says, for "Dr. Holmes had told her to make her husband . . . take an interest in things outside himself" (31). By focusing Septimus's perception on something outside of himself, Lucrezia hopes to engage him in dialogue with the world. It is a mode of perception that she is imposing, and it is because of her own sense of isolation that she does so.

There is a second instance in which Septimus is associated with the cloud-like and substanceless nature of meaning. The clouds have a "perpetual movement among them" (210). They change shape and meaning among them so that

> signs are interchanged, [and nothing is] fresher, freer, more sensitive superficially than the snow-white or gold-kindled surface; to change, to go, to dismantle the solemn assemblage was immediately possible; and in spite of the grave fixity, the accumulated robustness and solidity, now they struck light to earth, now darkness. (211)

With the same kind of movement and flux these formless clouds have, so too are the forms that Septimus perceives. The clouds seem to Septimus to be "going and coming, beckoning, signalling, so the light and shadow which now made the wall grey, now the bananas bright yellow" made the colors of the wall "glow and fade with the astonishing sensibility of some creature" (211). The forms have no meaning to Septimus and this is a symptom of his depression and insanity—though he sees that signs have no meaning in and of themselves, he is not capable of putting meaning into them. He cannot engage in the social consensus that creates meaning out of free-floating forms. If he could participate in the world outside of himself, he would be able to communicate and not be limited to the internal world he can only escape through suicide. His "mind stagnates without external ventilation" (*The Rambler* IV: 178) and he will "lose his days in unsocial silence, and live in the crowd without a companion" (IV: 364), as Johnson claims will happen when the writer remains in isolation.

Lucrezia's relationship with Septimus illustrates what occurs when there is talk but no conversation or communication. There is no presence of mind in Septimus's words, nor an attempt to place things in new perspectives. There is, in fact, nothing discussed. The beauty in the language is almost poetic. But Lucrezia cannot hear what Septimus hears, nor see the world that he sees. His isolation, his use of language, also creates her sense of isolation. The more they interact and the more they try to communicate, the further they move from each other. Lucrezia is always trying to transcribe his meanings, as those who believe language carries an inherent meaning will most faithfully do. But Septimus hears a number of voices, voices that have meaning to himself but do not communicate. Lucrezia writes his thought down "just as he spoke it. Some things were very beautiful; others sheer nonsense. And he was always stopping in the middle, changing his mind; wanting to add something; hearing something new; listening with his hand up. But she heard nothing" (212-13). He saw visions and faces of the dead, and it is the dead, his friend Evans, whom he is trying to reach. Septimus said people were "talking to him" and Lucrezia saw him only "talking to himself" (99). Without the voices of the outside world for Septimus to echo and incorporate into his language, he is left in his own solipsism, much in the same way the woman writer in *A Room* is left to speak to herself without a literary tradition to place herself.

The portrayal of Septimus's subjectivity, as something that is internal and where points of view are expressed in different voices and interact within the subject himself, is not a sympathetic one. Even Septimus knows that "communication is health; communication is happiness" (141), though, ironically, he is speaking to himself when he says it. Septimus cannot communicate because he is caught inside of his own subjectivity. The voices he hears are the voices of the dead, not the living, and therefore he is unable to participate in the active understanding that occurs between speaker and listener, where meaning is created out of free-floating forms.

An alternative to Septimus's mode of perception is one where multiple points of view or voices become focused on an object, rather than having the points of view trapped within the subject itself. This method is portrayed through the character Elizabeth Dalloway in the dinner-party section of the novel; Elizabeth's subjectivity is constructed through voices and points of view outside of herself. Lucy the maid, Clarissa's cousin Ellie Henderson, Sally Seton, Peter Walsh, Willie Titcomb, and Richard Dalloway all contribute to the reader's understanding of Elizabeth. However, through each perception we learn more about the subjectivity of the speaker than we do about Elizabeth.

Lucy initially reports how "Miss Elizabeth looked quite lovely; she couldn't take her eyes off her; in her pink dress, wearing the necklace Mr. Dalloway had given her" (252). Then Ellie Henderson asks herself if the young woman she is looking at isn't Elizabeth "grown up, with her hair done in a fashionable way, in the pink dress?" (257). We then find Ellie's own subjectivity entering into the perception: "But girls when they first come out didn't seem to wear white as they used . . . Girls wore straight frocks, perfectly tight, with skirts well above the ankles" (257). Ellie is reminded of her own lost youth and sexuality. She justifies her life by placing more value on what it meant to "come out" in her day than in the present. Isolated and alone, Ellie stands to the side passing judgement on the young and fertile Elizabeth.

We begin to hear the subjective voices of Sally Seton, Peter Walsh, and Willie Titcomb. Sally and Peter are discussing the marriage of Mr. and Mrs. Parry when Sally thinks, "And that very handsome, very self-possessed young woman was Elizabeth, over there, by the curtains, in red" (287). Sally's voice, tinged by her own boldness and sense of security, articulates Elizabeth's character as "self-possessed" and sees Elizabeth as wearing "red" instead of the muted and demure color pink that Ellie Henderson sees. Contrasting Sally's view is that of Willie Titcomb: "She was like a poplar, she was like a river, she was like a hyacinth" (287). Willie describes Elizabeth with natural metaphors, romanticizing her and perceiving her in terms he finds appealing, for he continues to say of Elizabeth, "Oh how much nicer to be in the country and do what she liked" (287). Immediately after this we find Peter Walsh's voice, saturated by his preoccupation with Clarissa, "She was not a bit like Clarissa" (287). There is also Peter's sense of experience, his awareness of the past and his youth, and how he is different from who he was: "There's Elizabeth, he said, she feels not half of what we feel, not yet" (295).

Finally, Elizabeth is defined in relation to her father, and as Sally says, "one can see they are devoted to each other" (295). And her father "had been looking at her . . . and he had thought to himself, who is that lovely girl? And suddenly he realized that it was his Elizabeth, and he had not recognized her, she looked so lovely in her pink frock" (295). Together "Richard and Elizabeth were glad [the party] was over, but Richard was proud of his daughter" (296). Each speaker sees Elizabeth and each thinks he or she knows who Elizabeth is, as though her outer appearance signifies her internal being. Though each speaker talks about Elizabeth, none of them see the same person. Each voice is rooted in its own particular subjectivity, and just as Septimus is limited to his own point of view and voice, and is therefore unable to construct a full identity based on communication and dialogue, so too are the identities of these speakers limited. The world they see—that is, their perceptions of Elizabeth—is a function of their internal perception. The voices do not interact with each other or show a shift and change as another perspective is introduced and contrasted with it. The subjectivities that these characters represent are static and do not maintain the fluid and dynamic movement on which meaning and identity, according to Woolf and Johnson, are based.

Both the modes of subjectivity represented by Elizabeth and Septimus lack the sense of communication that dialogue brings. In the case of Elizabeth, each voice is separated from every other voice, each reflects the subjectivity of the speaker, and all are unable to connect with the other. Septimus's voices do speak to each other, but they are caught within his subjectivity and unable to connect and make meaning of forms outside himself. In the character of Clarissa Dalloway we find communication and dialogue occurring between the voices of the internal self and the forms and symbols of the outside world. In fact, Clarissa's identity is so tightly bound to the world outside of herself that there is no real distinction between the two. There are two important passages that illustrate the multiplicity and split nature of Clarissa's identity. The first occurs while Clarissa thinks of Millicent Bruton, who has invited Clarissa's husband, Richard, to lunch. Clarissa "read on Lady Bruton's face" (44) the meaning of who she was. Lady Bruton becomes a mirror for how Clarissa perceives herself, and so Clarissa's identity is unknowable to herself without something outside of herself to reflect it.

What Clarissa sees in Bruton's face is "the dwindling of life" and her inability to absorb "the colours, salts, tones of existence she had been able to absorb in her younger years" (44). As Clarissa moves upstairs she feels "as if she had left a party, where now this friend now that had flashed back her face, her voice"; she shuts the door and finds herself "a single figure against the appalling night" or as a figure "against the stare of this matter-of-fact June morning" (45). It is paradoxical that what triggers Clarissa's feeling of isolation is seeing her face and hearing her voice reflected in her friends. Her figure that is seen as whole against the darkness or against the June day, is only seen as whole, and yet wholly alone, in relation to other people. Clarissa's sense of self is found outside of herself and this is further described by what she sees outside of her window: ". . . herself suddenly shrivelled, aged, breastless, the grinding, blowing, flowering of the day, out of doors, out of the window, out of her body and brain which now failed" (45). Clarissa experiences a lost sense of self, a self that is detached and separate from her perception, and is reflected in the world around her.

In a second passage we find Clarissa constructing her identity and composing a unified sense of self through her reflection. This passage shows the converging of the parts and elements of the self as Clarissa transfixes herself on the moment; she sees "the glass, the dressing table, and all the bottles afresh, collecting the whole of her at one point (as she looked into the glass), seeing the delicate pink face of the woman who was that very night to give a party; of Clarissa Dalloway; of herself" (54). Even Woolf's language illustrates the separation between "Clarissa" and "herself," and it is only through the objects that she views that she can pull the disparate elements together. Clarissa sees "her self—pointed; dartlike; definite" (55). The self she sees she knows is *not* the self she is, for the one she is aware of is the self "when some effort, some call upon her to be her self, drew the parts together." For "she alone knew how different, how incompatible and composed so for the world only into one centre, one diamond, one woman who sat in her drawing-room and made a meeting point" (55).

Clarissa's identity is a reflection of the world, and the world is a reflection of herself; at the same time, this reflexive identity allows Clarissa to unify, define, and distinguish herself from the rest of the world. The points of view that these images represent—Clarissa's friends looking at her, Clarissa looking at her friends, Clarissa looking at her reflection, the reflection staring back at Clarissa—begin to merge, each point of view dependent on the other for what it sees. It is this interdependence, this dialogue, that the subjectivities of Septimus and Elizabeth lack, for each in their own way are isolated without the kind of constructed meaning that Clarissa's identity maintains. This is the kind of subjectivity and meaning that Woolf advocates. Woolf's Common Reader is one who constructs the world in this way, framing objective meaning through subjectivity, while allowing subjectivity to be influenced and changed by the objective world. The Common Reader interprets by selecting what he or she chooses to reflect, and incorporates personal reflections into the interpretation. There is no real separation between the self and everything outside the self; one is always the repetition and echo of the other.

Unlike *Mrs. Dalloway*, *To the Lighthouse* deals with the sense of difference that occurs when there is an apparent separation between the self and the world. In this novel Woolf pursues her experimentation with dialogical subjectivity as she had defined it in Clarissa Dalloway by contrasting it to a subjectivity that is based on a unified sense of self, where identity is inherent to the subject and completely separate from the world around it. In *To the Lighthouse*, we find the desire for unity and connection, while identity is composed of the language and texts of the world. Identity as text and utterance is filled with the connotations of a split and fragmented world. Samuel Johnson's work on language in the Preface to the *Dictionary*, as well as his work on Locke, anticipate the split between words and meaning we find in Woolf's novels. The inability to fix the meaning of language, in order to create a sense of unity, echoes the lack of stable identity found in Woolf's characters.

Throughout the novel there is a constant drive toward wholeness and unity, and there is a desire to achieve this unity through language. Woolf demonstrates the impossibility of a complete identity, not by insisting on separation, difference, and fragmentation as the human condition, but by arguing that separation itself is nonexistent. As in the character of Clarissa Dalloway, we find subjectivity represented in *To the Lighthouse* as integrally connected to the objective world. This connection is based on a dialogic configuration, where all things are defined and constructed by the things they come into contact with. There is no distinction between self and world, subjective and objective, for each is dependent on the other, paradoxically, for its definition and distinction.[9]

Mrs. Ramsay, with her desire to bring people together, and Lily Briscoe, with her painting, try to establish a connection with the world. What Mrs. Ramsay dislikes about the people who surround her is the creation of difference when difference already exists: "Strife, divisions, difference of opinion, prejudices twisted into the very fibre of being . . . It seemed to her such nonsense—inventing differences, when people . . . were different enough without that" (17). The difference she perceives in the world around her also determines the structure of her identity. Not only is Mrs. Ramsay alienated from the world, but she is alienated from herself. If we understand Mrs.

Ramsay's subjectivity as we do Clarissa Dalloway's, then the difference or split Mrs. Ramsay experiences is merely a reflection of what she sees.

Woolf allows us to know this through the "Time Passes" section of the novel. The section as a whole is lyric, mourning the loss of the past, yet working toward the future. What the past represents is the illusion of wholeness and unity found, for most characters in the novel, as well as most readers of the novel, in Mrs. Ramsay. Woolf tells us the unity that is perceived is not real, but a reflection.

> That dream of sharing, completing, of finding solitude on the beach an answer, was then but a reflection in a mirror, and the mirror itself was but a surface glassiness which forms in quiescence when nobler powers sleep beneath. . . . to pace [the beach] was impossible; contemplation was unendurable; the mirror was broken. (202)

The mirror is broken, and so the reflection we find is distorted by chipped glass. The world we see is not whole, but fragmented and, therefore, so is our identity. What Mrs. Ramsay perceives — the reflection in the mirror — is split and fragmented. Though there is a desire for wholeness and unity, something that is believed to be found in the world outside of the self, what is found in the world is in fact a lack of unity and a sense of distortion. If Mrs. Ramsay's identity, and Clarissa's as well, is based on a dialogue with the world, then the fragmentation they find in themselves is a function of the fragmentation found outside of themselves. And, since the relationship between self and world is a dialogic one, the fragmentation found in the world is a function of the fragmentation found in the self. There is a sense of repetition in this dynamic, but we must keep in mind that there are an infinite number of interactions that the individual experiences. It is the different kinds of interactions that distinguish one mode of perception, one individual, from the other. Within these interactions there is no forward movement, for this implies an ultimate and unified end. There is only the shift and change of perception, interpretation, and meaning.

The split and fragmentation that Mrs. Ramsay perceives is reflected in her perception of the relationship she maintains with her life. There is an interactive relationship as Mrs. Ramsay sees herself as separate from her life, yet somehow connected to it.

> A sort of transaction went on between them, in which she was on the one side, and life was on another, and she was always trying to get the better of it, as it was of her; and sometimes they parleyed

(when she sat alone); there were, she remembered, great reconciliation scenes; but for the most part . . . she felt this thing that she
called life terrible, hostile, and quick to pounce on you if you gave
it a chance. (92)

Mrs. Ramsay maintains an antagonistic relation with her life, constantly
struggling with it, sometimes reaching agreement, but always moving in and
out of harmony with it. Her life itself is somehow separate from who she is.
But in this passage we find the process of dialogue—Mrs. Ramsay's understanding of who she is and the meaning of her life are constantly shifting and
changing. She never completely disconnects herself from "life," for if she
does her destiny would be similar to Septimus's. She recognizes the rift
between who she is and the experiences that make up her life, yet she maintains that tenuous and disturbing relationship with it, constantly struggling
to control and fix it, as Samuel Johnson tried to maintain and fix the meaning of language in his dictionary. Mrs. Ramsay, Johnson, and Woolf herself, all know the impossibility of keeping meaning stable, but they also
understand that it is the process of defining meaning and identity that is the
real end of their desire.

Lily Briscoe recognizes this same rift within herself, and her painting
reflects this and, therefore, her inability to find "some relation between those
masses" (221) is not a failed reflection, but a successful one. For Lily it is a
question of how "to connect this mass on the right hand with that on the left"
(83). She might connect the masses by "bringing the line of the branch
across so; or break the vacancy in the foreground by an object" (83). But the
danger, Lily senses, is "by doing that the unity of the whole might be broken"
(83). And though we know Lily has her "vision" at the end of the novel, the
unity she creates with "a line there, in the centre" (310) is artifice, arbitrary
and constructed by Lily herself—there is no center to the world.

Lily also creates her own center in her relationship with Mrs. Ramsay.
This is the cause of Lily's preoccupation with her, for she believes that Mrs.
Ramsay holds the truth of being, and Lily desires to become one with her.
Mrs. Ramsay is "like the treasures in the tombs of kings, tablets bearing
sacred inscriptions, which if one could spell them out, would teach one
everything" (79). Mrs. Ramsay becomes a text whose inscriptions Lily
hopes to read and understand. Again, we are reminded of Johnson's desire
to fix the English language and of his melancholy when he realizes it is
impossible. But it was "not knowledge but unity" (79) Lily desired, though
when she touched Mrs. Ramsay "nothing happened." What Lily desires is
that "razor edge of balance between two opposite forces" (287)—herself and

the world; she perceives the world as split and broken, and therefore her internal world is composed of that fragmentation. Like Mrs. Ramsay, whom Lily thinks represents wholeness, Lily feels "curiously divided, as if one part of her were drawn out there . . . the other [part] had fixed itself doggedly, solidly, here on the lawn" (234). This is because she sees herself in Mrs. Ramsay. It is not unity she sees but the fragmentation of which Mrs. Ramsay is composed.

Lily and Mrs. Ramsay share that "curiously divided" feeling. It is the fault of language, for it cannot bring completion to a sense of self and the world; language is too fluid and unstable, and no fixed meaning can ever be attached to it. For Lily "words became symbols, [and] wrote themselves all over the grey-green walls" (219). If only she could "put them together . . . write them out in some sentence, then she would have got at the truth of things" (219). Lily sees language as useless, "one could say nothing to nobody" (265). Words always "fluttered sideways and struck the object inches too low" (265).

Though Mrs. Ramsay and Lily are perceptive enough to see that language does play some role in the creation of the self, at least by seeing the impossibility of self-expression, neither is aware of the way language determines who they are. Language cannot function to express the internal and subjective self, mainly because there is no unified and settled self to express, and also because what we determine as individual and internal is *already* external. Our internal language is part of the external world; language does not inhabit us, but we inhabit language.

Woolf exhibits an awareness that internal language is a product of the external world, something she also understood in Johnson's work, through a moment of self-consciousness in her two characters: Mrs. Ramsay and Lily have thoughts that they don't recognize as their own, and each is surprised to find that she has thought it. The first instance occurs when Mrs. Ramsay is "sitting and looking, sitting and looking . . . until she became the thing she looked at" (97). She would concentrate upon some object she looked at, and some little phrase like "Children don't forget, children don't forget" would pop into her head, and then she would begin adding to it. After adding the phrases "It will end" and "It will come," she finds herself suddenly thinking, "We are in the hands of the Lord" (97). Mrs. Ramsay is instantly "annoyed with herself for saying that." She asks herself, "Who had said it? Not she; she had been trapped into saying something she did not mean" (97). It is the "insincerity slipping in among the truths" (98) that rouses her. She thinks words she does not mean and does not feel, words that are not her own but have become part of the way she expresses herself. We find Mrs. Ramsay's expression of her inner self composed of the outer world, making no real distinction between them.

The use of an outer language to construct an inner self is also found in Lily. Beginning the third section of the novel, "The Lighthouse," we find Lily asking herself, "What does it mean then, what can it all mean?" (217). The phrase itself, as Lily is well aware, is a "catchword" that is "caught up from some book, fitting her thought loosely, for she . . . could only make a phrase resound to cover the blankness of her mind" (217). Lily's mind is blank without the words from other texts, and she takes the clichéd phrase she has picked up from other books and uses it to construct her own life. Later in this section of the novel, Lily repeats the phrase, as though it were her own, no longer aware of it as coming from the outside, and using it as a way to understand life: "What does it mean? How do you explain it all?" (266). Even Lily's answers to these questions are not her own; in her thoughts, she answers these questions through Mr. Carmichael's language and point of view. His answer, which we get through Lily's consciousness, is "how 'you' and 'I' and 'she' pass and vanish; nothing stays; all changes; but not words, not paint" (267). What Lily perceives as her own words are foreign to her; she feels that one might say of her picture that it "remained for ever" but the "words spoken sounded even to herself, too boastful, to hint, wordlessly" (267).

None of Lily's thoughts and feelings belong to her, and this is further emphasized by the perception with which she sees herself as an artist.

> What was the good of doing it then, and she heard some voice saying she couldn't paint, saying she couldn't create, as if she were caught up in one of those habitual currents in which after a certain time experience forms in the mind, so that one repeats words without being aware any longer who originally spoke them. (237)

The words, women can't paint, women can't create, are Charles Tansley's words. It is through his point of view that Lily perceives herself as an artist. Just as she eventually uses the words, "what does it all mean," as though those thoughts originated in herself, so too does Lily's self-definition become the product of unconscious repetition of what others have told her about herself. Here Woolf illustrates what happens when the female artist has only the censoring voices of male companions to echo in her chamber of self-definition. The words of texts and the words of the world fill up and construct the identity, as the blankness of a writer's page is filled with the figures and ideas of the writers she has read.

The subjectivities that Lily and Mrs. Ramsay represent are split and fragmented—their voices and points of view are composed of the voices they hear and read. They are alienated and separated from themselves just as the world they perceive and reflect lacks unity. Communication occurs through the interaction of the various points of view, and within every statement and perception made there are at least two meanings—the meaning intended by the speaker, the meaning interpreted by the listener, and any other meaning that has been encoded into the statement as it passes from speaker to listener and is spoken again. Every statement has an internal dialogism, that is, it is overdetermined with meaning by the already spoken about,[10] and it is this double meaning of utterance that Woolf attempts to represent. What we find in *To the Lighthouse* are not the internal monologues of unified subjects, but the dialogues that create subjectivity itself.

The dialogic quality of utterance can be found throughout the novel, and an instance of this is in the conversation between Mrs. and Mr. Ramsay during their walk together. She wishes to tell him how much it will cost to mend the greenhouse, and instead talks about "Jasper shooting birds" (101). But Mrs. Ramsay's unobjectified thoughts continue after her husband's response: "Her husband was so sensible, so just. And so she said, 'Yes; all the children go through stages,' and began considering the dahlias in the big bed, and wondering what about next year's flowers" (101). Her response to Mr. Ramsay and her thoughts do not correspond. The meaning of her spoken words are full of meaning other than those the context of the conversation implies.

Mrs. Ramsay's consciousness as it is represented here illustrates the separation of meaning and language, where one can say what one does not mean or mean what one does not say. This is the split nature of utterance, where a speaker's words have many meanings at once, as well as having no meaning at all. This kind of communication is further represented in the dinner-party scene in "The Window" section of the novel. In this scene we find Woolf dialogizing the conversation, making the motivation and reception of utterances known to the reader, and allowing two conversations to occur at once. This narrative style, if looked at as traditional stream of consciousness, could be seen as concurrent monologues. However, the split nature of identity, as it has been described here, does not allow for a unified and central speaker. By viewing the narrative as dialogic, we begin to see that the split identity allows for split utterance. A speaker can say and think two opposing meanings simultaneously, in the same way Woolf splits her utterance between two speakers in her essay "Mr. Conrad: A Conversation." Though the dominating or central consciousness appears to be Mrs. Ramsay's, there is really no originating consciousness; there is only Mrs. Ramsay's commentary on the various points of view of the guests.

The passage begins with Mrs. Ramsay asking herself, "But what have I done with my life?" (125), as she directs each guest to his or her chair. As she looks at her guests she feels: "Nothing seemed to have merged. They all sat separate. And the whole of the effort of merging and flowing and creating rested on her" (126). Again we find Mrs. Ramsay perceiving the world around her as full of isolation and alienation, and we see her desire to place unity on all the separate consciousnesses. Also attached to her need to synthesize is the answer to her own question—her life has been spent filling the needs of other people, helping them to feel whole, complete, and connected to other people.

Ironically, however, as the dinner party proceeds, Mrs. Ramsay herself feels more and more detached and alienated from the scene she creates. She does not become fulfilled as she accomplishes her goal, but more lost, finding her words and voice in the words and voices of her guests. It is the same paradox found in Clarissa Dalloway, whose sense of isolation is increased as she sees her friends' faces and hears their voices reflected in her own. The movement toward unity for Mrs. Ramsay is the movement toward separation, and separation implies dialogue, for it is only through the momentary contact with each perspective that each speaker knows the boundaries of his own thoughts and feelings.

The dialogue between outer words and inner speech is the brief moment when characters know themselves.[11] Woolf contrasts the written dialogue given to each character with that character's, or some other character's, inner thoughts. For example, Mr. Bankes comments on the oddity "that one scarcely gets anything worth having by post, yet one always wants one's letters" (129). As commentary we receive Charles Tansley's thought, "What damned rot they talk," and Lily's thought that Tansley cleaned his plate as though "he were determined to make sure of his meals" (128). Here we have established a unique set of relationships based on the objectified thoughts of one character. The responses to Bankes's comment tell us more about the internal life of the other characters than they do about Bankes, much in the same way we learned about the characters in *Mrs. Dalloway* through Elizabeth Dalloway. It is the inner speech of each character in this novel that is revealed through the interaction with one character's outer speech. The outer speech, what one actually says out loud, does not necessarily correspond to what one means. Language, as it has been described, is not stable, and therefore literal or denotative meaning in communication is always unsure. All statements are dialogized statements, containing an infinite number of meanings. Communication comes from the dialogue that occurs between the connotations of language, not through the transparency of literal meaning. Just as Mrs. Ramsay and Lily say words that are not their own and which they do not mean, these speakers say words that have infinite meanings.

This interaction between inner and outer language occurs as Tansley, who is thinking how women have made "civilization impossible with all their charm," asserts out loud, "No going to the lighthouse tomorrow, Mrs. Ramsay" (129). Lily thinks that Tansley is "the most uncharming human being she had ever met" (130), and yet responds to him by saying, "do take me to the lighthouse with you. I should so love it" (130). Tansley knows that Lily's words are spoken to annoy him and he hates being "made fool of by women" (131), and so he responds abruptly that "it would be too rough for you tomorrow. You would be sick" (131). There are throughout this conversation, as Woolf is always trying to teach us, at least two levels of meaning, each interacting and determining the movement of the other. On the one hand we have Tansley asserting his authority by telling Mrs. Ramsay she will not go to the lighthouse, while it is his real dislike for women, not his concern for them, that motivates his comments. Similarly, it is Lily's dislike for Tansley, not her need to be taken care of, that causes her to ask him to be taken to the lighthouse. Lily knows that Tansley despises feminine charm, and so she uses whatever charm she has to provoke him.

Each speaker's language is determined by his or her subjective interpretation and motivation. The words that are heard are filtered and reprocessed to accommodate their own responses. Each point of view, each voice, represents a different language, while speakers talk at cross purposes though no one is aware — no one except Mrs. Ramsay, whose own subjective experience helps her to see the separation between the speakers. With her statement to Mr. Bankes, that he must "detest dining in this beer garden" (135), she calls on a common language for her guests to speak, filling her role as the constructor of unity. Woolf describes Mrs. Ramsay's use of language: "So, when there is a strife of tongues, at some meeting, the chairman, to obtain unity, suggests every one shall speak French . . . speaking French imposes some order, some uniformity" (135-36). The arbitrary choice of French, rather than English, as a common language chosen by Mrs. Ramsay, shows that social communication is based on social agreement, where all speakers should speak the same language and all words should mean the same thing. But social language is artificial, for the real nature of language is amorphous and fluid, containing a multitude of meaning in one response. Mr. Bankes replies to Mrs. Ramsay "in the same language" and even Mr. Tansley "who had no knowledge of the language, even spoke thus in words of one syllable" (136). Mrs. Ramsay controls her guests through her social language. She brings them together, if only momentarily, into the kind of harmony she desires.

As her guests become more and more adept at speaking the language she uses, Mrs. Ramsay detaches herself from the party she creates. Mrs. Ramsay, like Clarissa Dalloway, looks out the window and finds her sense of self. As she looks, "the voices [of her guests] came to her very strangely, as if they were voices at a service in cathedral, for she did not listen to the words" (166). She hears one voice after another, but none of them have any meaning; she does not know what the words mean, but "the words seemed to be spoken by her own voice, outside herself, saying quite easily and naturally what had been in her mind the whole evening while she said different things" (166). Though they use the language she has taught them, their voices are her voice, and with the many meanings attached to the perspectives that her guests represent, Mrs. Ramsay is able to say what she has been trying to say all night, more clearly and more definitely. Mrs. Ramsay finds her one voice in the many voices around her. It is impossible to get to know Mrs. Ramsay because she is composed of disparate perspectives and voices, but we can approach knowledge of her by considering each perspective in itself; we approach Mrs. Ramsay with the "fifty pairs of eyes" Lily desires to see her with. The "eyes" with which Lily views her are as varied as the "I's" that compose Mrs. Ramsay.

The interconnected, dynamic, interactive, and dialogic nature of identity preoccupied Woolf throughout her writing career. Many of the concepts and methods of analysis she used in her investigation were modeled after what she had found in her reading of Samuel Johnson. From the echo of a female literary history; to the madness that comes from stagnation and isolation; to the notion of identity as text, where the word and meaning are fluid, Johnson's ideas are part of the literary vocabulary she used to express both the critical and creative ways of thought. The novel form allowed her to investigate the various configurations of subjectivity and to see how the fluid movement of inner and outer worlds came together. The techniques used in *Mrs. Dalloway* and *To the Lighthouse* are not much different from those found in *A Room of One's Own*. In the novels the identities of the characters, their voices, and points of view, are made of perspectives and voices outside of themselves. There is no separation between self and world, but an intermingling. If the techniques of fiction and expository prose are similar, which of them represent a more "true" reality? The answer is both and neither, for, as we have seen, the authority upon which each genre is based is a construction, a putting together of unconnected perspectives through dialogue, interaction, and mingling of inner and outer worlds.

CHAPTER

·5·

Dialogue and Narrative:
The Waves, Three Guineas,
and *Between the Acts*

amuel Johnson's influence on Virginia Woolf is found not only in her notions of identity formation, but also on her narrative style and technique. As we have seen, identity formation is synonymous with the formation of narrative. In Woolf's late novels, *The Waves* (1931) and *Between the Acts* (1941), and her late essay *Three Guineas* (1938), we find Woolf describing the process of narration as the act of creating meaning by placing boundaries and limits. In these works Woolf develops literary forms that allow her to drop her authorial stance and to merge a number of voices and perspectives into a unique and ungrounded perspective that cannot be identified as belonging to Virginia Woolf. The author finally creates "eyeless" works, as she called *The Waves*, for in these final pieces there is no "I" to help unify the meaning of the novels or essay. Each of these defines and approaches the problem of subjectivity differently, though each constructs the concept of the subject through a dialogical configuration—that is, each utilizes the relation between inner and outer worlds. We come to understand that all stories, including literary history, are products of the voice that tells it, while that voice is also composed of numerous and varied voices.

Woolf combines the critical and creative to develop methods of narrative and storytelling that she had only begun to understand in her earlier work. Of all Woolf's novels, the form of *The Waves* preoccupied and troubled her the most. Throughout the diary we find Woolf struggling to articulate what she wishes to accomplish with the novel. At its conception, *The Waves*, initially entitled *The Moths*, was to fill out the "play-poem idea," where there would be "some continuous stream, not solely of human thought" (June 18 1927). A year later she refers to that "mystical eyeless book" (November 7, 1928) and her desire to write as a poet, "to saturate" language by somehow putting "practically everything in" (November 28, 1928). What Woolf searched for was some kind of narrative that would allow every aspect of experience to be represented simultaneously. She saw that it had some "vague yet elaborate design" that she found difficult to pull together: "whenever I make a mark I have to think of its relation to a dozen others" (October 11, 1929). This frustration is the same kind she experienced when trying to find the form of her first *Common Reader*. Then she knew that the form of an "Otway conversation," which she was considering, would "run away" with her because of the lack of closure such a form requires. In her writing of *The Waves* she felt compelled to connect every statement and image to every other she had made, making sure that the flexible quality of the narrative was sustained.

Woolf sensed the fragmentary nature of her work, and she likens the process to "only accumulating notes for a book" (November 30, 1929). In this comparison she stresses the process of composition and the desire to place form on disparity. Research for a book is merely the gathering of facts, all of which will only gain their meaning through the telling of the facts and the narrative used to place them in some order or form. The form she searches for is the search for a perspective or point of view that will help her to unify the various fragments: "From some higher station I may be able to pull it together" (November 30, 1929).[1] She begins to find the answer in the notion of conversation—and in this resolution we are again reminded of the "Otway conversation" she considered using to frame *The Common Reader*. To "pull it together," "comport it," "press it into one" she guesses that the end of *The Waves* "might be a gigantic conversation" (January 26, 1930). Again, she questions how to end the book, "save by a tremendous discussion, in which every life shall have its voice—a mosaic" (March 28, 1930). Eventually she sees *The Waves* as resolving into "a series of dramatic soliloquies" though the sense of difference and separateness that the soliloquy implies do not satisfy her. She wishes to "keep them running homogeneously in and out, in the rhythm of the waves" (August 20, 1930). The metaphor of the wave as a means for bringing unity to her novel recalls Johnson's metaphor for thought found in *The Rambler*. He describes thought as "rivulets issuing from distant springs" that unite with the "effervescence of contrary qualities" (V: 124); the image of water allows both writers to communicate the paradox of difference and synthesis in one stroke.

The problem of the "eyeless" book is the problem of writing an "I-less" narrative, where the author effaces the omniscient narrator and allows the mosaic of voices to interact and blend on their own. Conversation becomes one of the only means of solving this problem, but as she tells us, she has still not "mastered the speaking voice" (March 28, 1930). And so we find Woolf adopting a metaphor — the waves — to represent a kind of interaction and relation she found so difficult to express. Much in the same way as the Common Reader is a metaphor for the rhetoric of the essays, so too are the waves representations, not only of the content of the novel, but of the form, purpose, and method of the prose she uses to articulate that content. That is, *The Waves* is about its own narration.

Early critics of *The Waves* best understood the form of the novel to be a series of characters, not speaking to one another, but as six interweaved soliloquies, thereby taking Woolf's word that each section is a dramatic monologue. Others have tried to describe the form in terms of music, opera, lyric, or as a reflection of her preoccupation with perception itself.[2] Though there is a dramatic element in the form Woolf uses, and though it could be argued that she tried to absorb the qualities she admired in the Elizabethan dramatists, it is not the form of the monologue that she ultimately strived for. As she tells us, the breaks between monologues created too much waste and did not allow for homogeneity. What Woolf found so appealing about the dramatic form is its lack of an omniscient or guiding narrator; in drama a narrative perspective can only be deduced through the interaction of dramatic voices.[3] We can assume that any one dramatic voice belongs to the author, that there is some mechanism that can record inner experience, and that through this perspective or mechanism we can ground any interpretation, but this assumption will always remain in the realm of conjecture.

The Waves is not a narrative in search of a guiding voice, but a narrative in search of voices.[4] Each of the six voices in the novel — Neville, Bernard, Louis, Rhoda, Susan, Jinny — are concerned with finding some unity and meaning to their lives and identities. Their words echo the problems of constructing a single narrative. Each voice is detached and ungrounded, without a context to place it or a purpose for the spoken words. That is, each voice is a speech act motivated for no known reason and directed to no understood audience.[5] The notion of audience, especially in the later part of Woolf's career, preoccupied her: How does one write without an audience? These voices, however, speak without an audience. It could be that each voice is, in fact, speaking to itself, not with a unified voice that expects no response, but as a split inner voice, or identity, that contains more than one perspective. Each voice is a microcosm of the larger narrative that contains it.

Throughout the novel there are constant allusions to the split nature of identity, the way it is composed and constructed by sources outside of the self, and the desire to create meaning and order through forms and patterns. Bernard's voice articulates the narrative strategy of the novel most clearly. As Bernard states early on, "the complexity of things becomes more close" and then it becomes clear to him that he is "not one and simple, but complex and many." Bernard in "public, bubbles; in private, is secretive" (76). Bernard's definition of himself echoes Penelope Otway's description of Conrad, who is not "one and simple; no, he is many and complex" ("Mr. Conrad" 78). In that essay Woolf attempts to define the modern writer and to argue that it is the great writer who can bring those particularly opposite selves in relation to one another. This is what Woolf attempts to do in *The Waves*. Bernard finds he has to "effect different transitions; [has] to cover the entrances and exits of several different men who alternately act their parts as Bernard. . . . at the moment when I am most disparate, I am also integrated" (76-77). Bernard's identity, as he explains it, is composed of several different men who "act" their parts when called upon. This process is similar to that of Clarissa Dalloway who pulls herself together when "some call upon her to be her self" (55) is required. Woolf's paradox of identity is most clearly expressed through Bernard's statement that he is "most disparate" when he is "also integrated." His sense of identity is grounded in the disparity of his parts. In the same way, the unity or identity of *The Waves* is found in the disparity of voices of which it is composed.

The voice of Neville finds it difficult to integrate itself: "I do not know myself sometimes, or how to measure and name and count out the grains that make me what I am" (83). He finds it painful to be "recalled, to be mitigated, to have one's self adulterated, mixed up, become part of another. As he approaches I become not myself but Neville mixed with somebody—with whom?" (83). Neville's perception reflects that of the reader who cannot tolerate the diversity of which an open narrative is composed. This is because with the lack of stable form, which does bring a sense of freedom, there is a lack of control. If Neville, and the reader, cannot depend on an identity that is consistent, then who or what will that identity be each time it is encountered? Identity is a text with the fluid meaning of its symbols.

Louis, in comparison, desires the sense of merging that Neville wishes to avoid, yet Louis cannot accept the sense of difference and separation. He imitates the English accent of his friends, not wanting it to be known that he is from Australia. He marries a woman with a cockney accent, thinking it will make him feel part of a group of outsiders, but he is only teased by those of his wife's class for being pretentious. No matter what he does, he is known as "an alien, external" (94). He is aware "of hats bobbing up and down in perpetual disorder," though he is determined to "reduce" them "to order" (94). Louis, another kind of reader, is the perpetual outsider, who tolerates his position of otherness by constantly trying to unify it and bring coherence. He does not fear a sense of lost identity, as Neville does, but desires to merge with others in order to escape his separateness.

Louis cannot see himself except through the form and order he finds in the world around him. He constantly desires to be like those he perceives himself to be most different from, those who are self-contained and self-defined. However, his desire for similarity only functions to make him more different. Louis finds existence without relationships and on the outside unbearable. He sees pattern and order in other people's lives: "'Susan has children; Neville mounts rapidly to the conspicuous heights. Life passes. . . . I do this, do that, and again do this and then that. Meeting and parting, we assemble different forms, make different patterns'" (170). Louis needs to "nail these impressions to the board and out of the many men in me make one" (170), for if he does not, he feels he shall "fall like snow and be wasted" (170). What Louis fears is the sense of annihilation and obscurity that Septimus Smith suffers from. Like the reader who gains his authority by limiting his interpretation to a definitive one, Louis feels he will gain control and significance by stabilizing his identity, rather than fade into nothingness.

The compact unity that Louis strives for is the desire for meaning through form and order. This desire manifests itself differently through the various voices in the novel. Susan, for instance, envies Jinny's ability to bring order with her presence. As Jinny enters the restaurant where all meet for a reunion, Susan notes: "'She stands in the door. Everything seems stayed. . . . She seems to centre everything . . . like rays round the star in the middle of a smashed window-pane. She brings things to a point, to order'" (12). Susan desires what she does not have and what she believes others possess. The unity in Jinny's world is something that Susan projects and creates for Jinny. Jinny's ability to create order around her is Susan's construction, a unity that can only be found in the world outside herself.

Susan cannot determine who she is at all. She is genderless and lacks specificity; in her, there is merging but not difference. "But who am I," she sometimes thinks, "I am not a woman." Like Neville, she finds it difficult to merge with other people. She cannot "float gently, mixing with other people" (96) and she does not even try, instead finding her place in nature where she identifies with the unified cycles of "the seasons." Instead of dealing with the paradox of unity and diversity in defining herself, she finds a kind of unity by identifying completely with something outside of herself: cycles of nature, which move through consistent and predictable patterns.

The lack of pattern or order is suffered most acutely by Rhoda who, also like Septimus Smith, has no sense of self, and because of this eventually commits suicide. She finds her old friends as somehow connected to each other because they are each connected to something else.

> I perceived, from your coats and umbrellas, even at a distance, how you stand embedded in a substance made of repeated moments run together; are committed, have an attitude, with children, authority, fame, love, society; where I have nothing. I have no face. (222-23)

Rhoda too sees form and unity in things outside herself, and she has not the security of the repeated moment. Because of this she has "nothing," "no face," no identity, no eyes with which to see herself reflected.[6] Without the "repeated moments," the echoes of voices to create patterns, there is no chamber in which Rhoda can gain something for herself to construct her identity. Isolated and removed from the world around her, Rhoda's suicide, just as Septimus's, is the ultimate act of defiance, where she is no longer separate from, but eternally connected to, the universe.

How does the voice know itself when identity is something it is always separated from? Though identity is "I-less," like *The Waves* itself, it has the benefit of the "eyes" of others. Like Mrs. Ramsay, who one needs fifty pairs of eyes to know, Bernard feels that to know himself he needs "the illumination of other people's eyes" (116). He needs that illumination because he is "traversing the sunless territory of non-identity" (116). With people he is "many-sided" and is relieved from "darkness" (116) of his separation and isolation. His eyes are a "thousand eyes of curiosity" (143) since his identity is part of those who surround him.

Someone like Louis, on the other hand, cannot stand the "illumination, reduplication" that the eyes of others bring to him, though he realizes he cannot avoid the gaze of others who define who he is. He desires unity and focus to understand himself, yet the disparate nature of his being is always there to haunt him. He etches his name to gain permanence and stability: "'I have signed my name' . . . 'already twenty times. I, and again I, and again I. Clear, firm, unequivocal, there it stands, my name. Clear-cut and unequivocal am I too'" (167). However, he realizes that "packed" inside himself is "a vast inheritance of experience" (167). But for the moment, as Clarissa Dalloway, who sees herself in the glass, Louis tells us, "I am compact; now I am gathered together this fine morning" (167).

Bernard, in contrast, is ambivalent about the role of structure and form in his self-definition. This is because, as the story-teller, he is aware of both the lack of order in reality and the necessity of placing an artificial structure on it through language. But Bernard has difficulty finding order and form, just as Woolf struggled to find the form of *The Waves*. Bernard will not allow himself to be seduced by the illusion of coherence. At one moment we find Bernard saying that he has been born "knowing that one word follows another" (132) and therefore "finding sequences everywhere" he cannot "bear the pressure of solitude" (132). At another moment he feels the "sequence returns; one thing leads to another—the usual order" (155). And yet, he says, "I still resent the usual order. I will not let myself be made to accept the sequence of things" (155). The "sequences" Bernard sees are the "repeated moments" that Rhoda cannot find for herself. Bernard cannot bear the pressure of solitude because he knows how important those patterns are to constructing his meaning and identity. At the same time, he resists "the usual order" for this is the same impulse Louis has to "nail these impressions to the board" to make himself one and unified. Finally, Bernard is aware of how those with whom he comes into contact help to define the structure of his identity. At Hampton Court he sees Susan, Louis, Rhoda, Jinny, and Neville standing at the door, and he knows that when he joins them "another arrangement will form, another pattern" (210). Though he has yet to join them he already feels "the order of my being changed" (210). Bernard most clearly understands the function of the other in defining the self, and his ambivalence proves it. He does not fear the power of the other to change his form as Rhoda does, and therefore does not withdraw completely into the world of nonidentity. Nor does he fear the flux created between self and other, including the sense of exclusion that accompanies it, as Louis does. Instead he investigates the nature of this dynamic and its relation to his desire to make stories. This is what the final section of the novel is about, devoted to Bernard, who functions to place structure onto the novel as a whole.

The final section reveals that Woolf attempted to master the "speaking voice" while at the same time placing everything within a "gigantic conversation." What Bernard discovers, as does Woolf, is that the boundaries that are created through structure and form are a function of the world outside the self. Earlier in the novel Bernard tells us, "But soliloquies in the back streets soon pall. I need an audience. That is my downfall. That always ruffles the edge of the final statement and prevents it from forming" (115). Here, the other with whom Bernard merges and defines himself is articulated as the "audience." The audience, on which he depends, keeps him from achieving a sense of closure and unity; he cannot form a final statement. As the writer and storyteller, "Different people draw different words from me" (134). Whom he speaks to, whom he comes into contact with, will determine which words he says and which story he tells. In the last section of the novel there is a specific, constructed, implied audience that allows Bernard to form the words that help him to create meaning in his life.

The section begins with Bernard telling his audience that he is going to "sum up." He uses second person, speaking to a specific listener whom he describes and gives a context for.

> "Now to explain to you the meaning of my life. Since we do not know each other (though I met you once I think on board a ship going to Africa) we can talk freely. The illusion is upon me that something adheres for a moment . . . is completed. This, for the moment, seems to be my life. If it were possible, I would hand it you entire. . . . But unfortunately, what I see . . . you do not see. You see me, sitting at a table opposite you, a rather heavy, elderly man, grey at the temples. . . . But in order to make you understand, . . . I must tell you a story . . . stories of childhood, stories of school, love, marriage, death . . . and none of them are true. . . . how I distrust neat designs of life that are drawn upon half sheets of notepaper." (238)

Unlike the rest of the novel, the act of communication in this section is directed to a specific audience, and placed within a context that allows us to understand the purpose of the utterance. The reader finds it easy to identify with the stated audience, and so when Bernard explains that he is going to give "the meaning of my life," though "we do not know each other," we take it as an invitation to understand the meaning of the novel. The events that constitute his life and the story he can tell to describe them would make up one of the "neat designs" or patterns he refuses to submit himself to. But this story is also the narrative of his identity and the interpretation of what it all means.

The process through which this "speaking voice" of Bernard puts the fragments of his life together is the same process by which the fragments of a book are made into one narrative. The ambivalence that Bernard feels toward the idea of order and form is reflected in his opening words in the final section of the novel. The fact that something "adheres for a moment" and is "completed" is viewed by Bernard as an "illusion," and it is this illusion of completeness that is his life. He knows that what he sees, we do not see, and that to help us to understand the meaning of his life he must tell us "stories." Like Woolf, he must make up the stories while distrusting the very designs he develops to communicate the meaning of his identity and life.

For Bernard there are at least two things operating in the construction of identity—there is the desire for order and form, and the separation, merging, and mixing of our identity with the world. Bernard points out the difference between himself and his friends, each of whom "suffered terribly as we became separate bodies" (241). Each exists, "not only separately but in undifferentiated blobs of matter" (246). In their separation there is a similarity, for it is only in relation to one another that they can define their separateness. What Bernard calls "my life" is not "one life" that he looks back upon: "'I am not one person; I am many people; I do not altogether know who I am—Jinny, Susan, Neville, Rhoda, or Louis: or how to distinguish my life from theirs'" (276). The identity of the individual, like the identity of the writer who exists within a literary tradition, is composed of many people. It is impossible to distinguish one writer or individual from the multitude of writers or individuals that writer has come into contact with. The conundrum exists in the "contact of one with another" (281), and, as Bernard states earlier in the novel, "[w]e are forever mixing ourselves with unknown quantities" (118). Bernard, the constructor of narrative, explains the process of influence that Woolf is subject to. She herself has mixed the "unknown quantities" of Johnson and Stephen, just as the writers in her female literary tradition will mix with theirs.

The problem of defining the self is in defining the boundaries between our self and what is not our self. Woolf evokes the Paterian analogy of likening art to music by describing how the identities in the novel interact with each other.[7]

> How impossible to order them rightly; to detach one separately, or to give the effect of the whole. . . . What a symphony, with its concord and its discord and its tune on top and its complicated bass beneath, then grew up! Each played his own tune, fiddle, flute, trumpet, drum or whatever the instrument might be. (256)

If for Pater music represents the ideal merging of form and content, of subject and expression, then for Woolf this unity and wholeness is constructed from the separate voices or instruments that make it up. It is difficult to distinguish voices, to tell which comes first or what it sounds like alone, for each instrument finds its sound and form in relation to every other instrument. In literary history, each writer finds his or her identity and form within the symphony of voices, full of harmony and cacophony, of which the writer is a part.

The act of telling stories, of placing meaning on experience, is the act of placing boundaries and limits. We are told that "if there are no stories, what end can there be, or what beginning? Life is not susceptible perhaps to the treatment we give it when we try to tell it" (267). The "true order of things" is our "perpetual illusion" (271). So we "pretend that life is a solid substance, shaped like a globe, which we turn about in our fingers" and we "pretend that we can make out a plain and logical story, so that when one matter is despatched . . . we go on, in an orderly manner, to the next" (251). The logic of understanding ourselves and others is an illusion of substance. Literary history too is a perpetual illusion of solid substance, where we articulate a plain and logical story. The history of literary influence in which I place Woolf, with Johnson and Stephen as two points of contact, is as much a function of my narrative and the limits and boundaries I set up, as would be the female literary history Woolf projects in *A Room of One's Own,* and the feminist literary histories that narrate Woolf's experience as a woman writer. And Woolf would be the first to acknowledge this.

Woolf gives form to *The Waves* in the same way that Bernard gives form to his life—each tells a story, an artificial boundary that creates meaning. At the same time, the voice that tells that story is not unified. Bernard is composed of the many people he comes into contact with, while Woolf's authorial perspective is never clear. Woolf has split her voice or perspective among the various voices of the novel, all of whom compose Bernard, but none of whom help us to know who Bernard or Woolf really are or what they really think and feel. In *The Waves* Woolf develops a narrative technique that allows her to achieve a kind of unity without a unifying perspective, and it is this technique that makes the novel an aesthetic success.[8] This strategy calls attention to the artificiality of the speaking "I" in the text, and Woolf exploits the use of this "I" in her next major work of the period, *Three Guineas.*

Three Guineas has been read as one of Woolf's most polemic and political works. While some critics have focused on the socioeconomic themes, others have begun to explain the use of narrative strategies to subvert the authority and tyranny Woolf critiques.[9] In *Three Guineas* the "I" of the narrative is problematic. Woolf creates her audience and draws on the experience and writing of other sources to establish the authority of the speaking "I." While in *A Room of One's Own* she bases a history on fiction, using the voices of the three Marys, in *Three Guineas* she bases fiction on fact. The dialogue between the academic and scholarly footnotes and the speaker of the essay, as well as the embedded voices within her narrative, create a cacophony of voices within which the reader is to extract meaning. We find Woolf examining the relationship between the speaker and the spoken to, and how the identity of the "I" is determined by its audience.

The essay is not only a series of letters, but letters within letters, so the person to whom she speaks constantly shifts, while at the same time remaining on the level of the hypothetical. Here the stability of the audience is called into question, and if, like Bernard, "different people draw different words" from Woolf, the shifting audience is necessary. Her words and voices are not only a function of the audience to whom she speaks, but it also consists of the voices found in the biographies and histories she quotes. The apparatus to the text complicates things further; though the notes are composed of actual historical texts, they are appended to a work that verges on fiction. Also, the explication that occurs in each note is often long and detailed, contributing yet another voice to the cacophony of voices within the work. The notes give the work a the same Menippean quality of colloquy that is found in Johnson's *Dictionary*. Woolf uses the language of those she is trying to criticize—i.e., traditional academic discourse—to create a sense of drama and conversation, and persuade those who represent institutional structures to see things from her point of view.[10]

As the essay begins, we discover that there are at least two audiences whom she is addressing—an actual and an implied audience. The "I" defines the implied reader of her text, so that her actual readers may understand to whom she is responding. The speaker tells the reader how she will proceed: "Let us draw what all letter-writers instinctively draw, a sketch of the person to whom the letter is addressed" (3). With much the same language that Bernard uses to describe himself, the audience of this letter, of the text as a whole, is "a little grey on his temples; the hair is no longer thick on the top of [his] head. . . . There is nothing parched, mean or dissatisfied in [his] expression. . . . [He has] never sunk into the contented apathy of middle life" (3). Like the speaker herself, the recipient is from the "educated class," and they both speak with the same accent, can talk without difficulty about war and peace, politics and people, and they both earn their own livings. But there is a gulf so "deeply cut" between them that she has been unable to find the words to respond to his question, "How in your opinion are we to prevent war?" (3)

The speaker immediately calls on Mary Kingsley to speak for her. Kingsley's words become the speaker's words, and Woolf's voice is then composed of the voices that have come before her, creating the kind of literary history she discusses in *A Room of One's Own.* Kingsley tells us, "I don't know if I ever revealed to you the fact that being allowed to learn German was *all* the paid for education I ever had" (4). We are told that Kingsley is not only speaking for herself, but for many of the "daughters of educated men"; and she is not only speaking for them, but pointing out a very important fact about them: all family funds went toward educating the sons, not the daughters.

Woolf adds a footnote to this passage on Mary Kingsley that helps to characterize the audience further. The note, and the quotations inside it, also place other layers onto a voice that is speaking for the narrator. This note is not intended for the implied reader who is "a little grey," but is addressed to the actual reader who is interested in the history of women's education. Woolf tells us that Kingsley's experience speaks for many women, and she uses the footnote to tell us more explicitly about the history that underlies Mary's words. In it we read about Anne Clough and Elizabeth Haldane. Haldane's words, which Woolf quotes, lead to the idea that women in the nineteenth century were encouraged to remain ignorant. And if they were not ignorant, it was thought best that they simulate ignorance. Woolf also quotes Thomas Gisborne, from his *On the Duties of Women,* where he argues that women should not simulate ignorance of the world, for dissimulation is unethical. Within the note, a voice separate from the voice of Kingsley, Woolf quotes other writers, using the quotation marks that literally signify that the language belongs to someone else. The voices in the quotes compose the voice of the note, which composes Kingsley's voice, which composes the narrator's voice. All these voices contribute to the narrator's statement by showing the reader the social, political, and cultural background in which all women, at least historically, are raised, and her statement addresses why there is such a great chasm between the speaker and her implied reader — the social expectations of each as man and woman are quite different. The approach we find to the idea of a chamber of female voices in *Three Guineas* is distinguished from *A Room* in that here Woolf tries to mimic and represent the narrative process. In *A Room* she deconstructs the speaking "I" and calls attention to its rhetorical composition, but she does not present an option for using it as a viable technique to critique the culture in which she lives. In *Three Guineas* she presents an audience by embedding voices and by problematizing the audience instead.

The structure of the essay as a whole also complicates the notion of audience while simultaneously incorporating other dialogic elements. She has left the letter from the implied reader unanswered for three years, and part of the purpose of her response is to justify her lack of communication by illustrating how complicated the issue really is. She does this by placing letters within her letters, allowing other voices and points of view to enter her text. At moments, she places dialogue within the secondary letters, creating a multitude of relationships between the various audiences involved.

The implied reader, the man with the "grey hair" with whom the narrator identifies, is a function of all the other audiences found in the narrative. In a dialogic relationship, voices are not only composed of other voices, but voices interact with a range of audience. An example of this is the letter the speaker presents to illustrate the poverty of women's colleges. She has received an appeal from the honorary treasurer of a women's college, and talking to her implied reader she says that the problem of addressing the treasurer is that she must dictate the terms of her gift. The speaker begins to "draft a letter to her" while writing the implied reader. The narrator no longer addresses the implied reader, but the treasurer to whom her letter is addressed. In the draft it is stipulated that the treasurer will only receive a guinea if she will use it "to produce the kind of society, the kind of people that will help to prevent war" (33). She then goes on to describe the kind of education that is needed, and then we are told that "the letter broke off there" (35). By ending the letter so abruptly, the narrator, and Woolf, call attention to the artificial nature of narration and the meaning it claims to express.

Woolf begins to break the audience down into different kinds of audiences, each of which is a function of the other; Woolf's reader is a function of the implied reader, who is a function of the treasurer to whom the letter is addressed. Just as the narrator is composed of a variety of voices, so too is the audience or reader. The letter ends not because there is a lack of things to say but because "the face on the other side of the page—the face that a letter writer always sees—appeared to be fixed with a certain melancholy" (35). The writer hears her auditor's response and is unable to continue her argument.

The points that Woolf and her narrator are trying to make are spoken by the treasurer who is the audience of the unfinished letter. In the treasurer's words, the narrator speculates what the response will be. The treasurer will ask, the narrator tells us, "'What is the use of thinking how a college can be different . . . when it must be a place where students are taught to obtain appointments?'" "'Dream your dreams . . . fire off your rhetoric, but we have to face realities'" (35). The treasurer will tell her that she is not being practical because students must be able to get appointments when they leave college. The writer imagines that the treasurer tells her that she is full of rhetoric, which in fact she is.

The speaker's response to these statements is directed toward her implied reader. She understands that the "reality" to which the treasurer refers is that of money—students must be taught to earn their livings. And therefore this school for the daughters of educated men must be constructed along the same lines as the schools for the sons, and therefore we will never be able to teach people to prevent war. However, the speaker proceeds to argue for an alternative education, and her argument is directed toward her implied reader, not the treasurer. She uses the letter to the treasurer as a vehicle for discussing the issues that guide the entire essay.

Three Guineas complicates the notion of audience, and though this is one of Woolf's most polemical essays, it is not one of her most direct. She constructs the identity of the speaker by creating at least two audiences, the implied and the actual, using the voices of other texts, both within the body of the essay and in the footnotes, and by placing letters within the letter, creating a variety of dialogues between herself and the recipient. The ambiguity of narrative authority is the same kind found in *The Waves*, and, like *The Waves*, *Three Guineas* shows us the interdependence of voices in the text— each narrative voice is composed of voices both within and outside of itself. It also makes the relationship to the audience ambiguous, destabilizing all elements in the processes of reading and writing.

Like *Three Guineas* and *The Waves*, which define the elements that construct the "I" and its relation to its audience, *Between the Acts* investigates the same interdependency. But unlike the other works, *Between the Acts* concentrates on the identity of the audience more fully than the speaking "I," and it attempts to describe the effect language has on the audience's perception of itself. Miss La Trobe is metaphor, or trope, for the language maker, and she evokes responses in her audience that cause them to look at themselves in different ways. As the responses La Trobe creates change and vary, so too does her relationship and response to her audience. Miss La Trobe is as dependent on her audience for the meaning of her work, through the audience's ability to understand, as the members of the audience are dependent upon her for their understanding of themselves.[11]

Woolf's first approach to this novel, as it had been in the earlier works, was to the question of form.[12] Her journal tells us that the only hint she has toward the next novel is that "it's to be dialogue: and poetry: and prose; all quite distinct" (July 19, 1937). Typically, Woolf attempts to break down the notion of genre, to have all genres interact so that no one determines the ultimate form. She finally sets out to accomplish what she had set out in *Three Guineas* and *The Waves*: to rid the narrative of a domineering and dominating "I" through which all characters and events are interpreted and defined.

Instead of the pronoun "I" there shall be "we": "but 'I' rejected: 'We' sub-stituted: to whom at the end there shall be an invocation? 'We' . . . composed of the many different things . . . we all life, all art, all waifs and strays—a rambling capricious but somehow unified whole" (April 26, 1938). The singular unified whole is composed of the plural "we," as are life, art, and people. Structure in this form is not predictable and established, but rather has a logic of its own that Woolf herself cannot define. The dialogic form, as it evolved in Woolf's work, is organic in that it allows entities to merge and separate, to be singular and plural, to be the self and other. It is this rela-tionship that Woolf exploits in her novel.

Between the Acts is a novel based on the dialogic form.[13] It is about the pro-duction of dramatic dialogue, both on the literal level of producing a pageant and on a figurative level of producing dialogic interaction between the audi-ence and the text of Miss La Trobe's play, and between the reader and *Between the Acts*.[14] It is also about the construction and impact of literary his-tory. Through La Trobe's narrated history the audience finds its place and meaning in the present moment. In this work we find the interaction of inner and outer worlds that aids in the creation and understanding of experience, and as Guiguet explains, the "collective experience of a whole culture . . . remains spread out in historic time and is only introduced into the present from the outside" (323). The individual consciousness has no existence, and it is this dispersal of point of view that causes a sense of obscurity in the novel. The novel utilizes images of conversation and dialogue to represent the lack of a central and domineering consciousness. It begins and ends with images of conversation that frame an otherwise open-ended narrative. The first scene recalls the setting of a drama, "It was a summer's night and they were talking" (3), while it ends with a sense of beginning again, "The cur-tain rose. They spoke" (21). Speech is the dominant image and represents the importance of dialogue in the structure of the novel.

Unlike Woolf's previous works, however, *Between the Acts* is the most met-alinguistic, with imagery of dialogue and language commenting explicitly on the construction of identity and meaning. The action of the novel rests in the interaction between the audience and the play, and behind the play, Miss La Trobe, manipulating and controlling the audience's perception of itself. La Trobe's manipulation should not be considered the point of view or con-sciousness through which we are to interpret the novel. The lack of mediation found in the dramatic form is emphasized by the fact that La Trobe is hidden from her audience who is often unable to pinpoint her voice and her position.

The audience is understood as a group of dispersed, cacophonic, and anonymous voices. Through this representation of audience we get a clearer understanding of what Woolf was doing with audience in *Three Guineas*. The audience, like the reader and the writer, is broken down into numerous points of view. It is not the personality of each voice that is important, but each voice's role in relation to every other voice. We are given the voices of the characters as they are heard from a perspective outside of subjectivity. It is not the internal monologue that is stressed, but the dialogue and dynamic between points of view, the process itself.

Without some middle ground, like the text and drama itself, the voices do not form the dialogic relationship that creates meaning. And so, as in the following passage, we find the voices separated from each other, forming no unified sense: "Across the hall a door opened. One voice, another voice, a third voice came wimpling and warbling: gruff—Bart's voice; quavering—Lucy's voice; middle tone—Isa's voice. Their voices impetuously, impatiently, protestingly came across the hall" (37). These voices are detached, not in conversation and interaction. The voices of an audience that doesn't know what to do with itself ring aimlessly and meaninglessly. It is the voice of Septimus Smith that we hear, a voice that is unable to connect to the world around it.

Miss La Trobe presents to the audience at Pointz Hall the yearly pageant. Between the acts of the play and moments of literary history are various intervals, times when the audience mingles and when Woolf allows her reader to see how the text of the play affects the perception and inner thoughts of the audience. In fact, we find members of the audience can only relate to each other in terms of the play, without it, they are void of language. The play becomes text, a system of symbols and signs, and mediates the voices and perspectives that would otherwise remain dispersed in the air.

During the first interval the music chants a theme that runs through the novel: "Dispersed are we" (95). This phrase is repeated over and over as the audience stirs and separates into a group of unconnected individuals, unlike the unified mass they represent when watching the play. Once the first act ends, the audience "streamed, spotting the grass with colour, across the lawns, and down the paths" (96). There is a sense of misdirection in this image; without the play the audience disperses into chaotic movement. The audience enters the barn for tea, and what Woolf stresses in this scene is the fragmentary, anonymous, and unrelenting emptiness of the voices. Mrs. Manresa speaks to the company in her "public voice" (102), while Mrs. Swithin, "ignoring the fact that she spoke to the empty air" (103) repeats the fact that the birds come every year from Africa. As the barn fills, "[f]umes rose. China clattered; voices chattered" (103).

Isa, the hostess of the pageant, maneuvers her way to the table, and her words are the words of the drama she has been watching, "Dispersed are we" (103). The language of her inner world, like Mrs. Ramsay and Lily Briscoe, is the world of outer speech. The play becomes part of how Isa organizes her world. The "noise of china and chatter" drown out her murmur as she listens to the detached and unnamed voices around her talking of tea and milk and of the king and queen going to India. Finally, when the identified voice of William Dodge steps up beside her she can say, "It's the play. . . . The play keeps running in my head" (105).

When the audience begins to reassemble, their voices still chatter. As they sit the "other voice," the "inner voice" (119) of each begins to speak. It is at this transition, from between the acts to the act itself, that the subjectivity of the audience begins to emerge. But without the play to focus on, without the interaction with language, the audience turns from their inner voices back to their empty chatter. The "stage was empty. . . . The audience turned to one another and began to talk" (120). Here is the distinction that Samuel Johnson made between talk and conversation. There is no meaning in talk, no substance, only the endless chatter of empty words that do not create meaning or understanding.

Miss La Trobe, unlike the others, hears the discord that the voices create. She is detached from them, and by gaining a distance and perspective she can manipulate the fragmentary composition. Hidden behind the bushes, La Trobe hears the voices in a context that reveals the lack of personality and subjectivity: "Over the tops of the bushes came stray voices, voices without bodies, symbolical voices they seemed to her, half hearing, seeing nothing, but still, over the bushes, feeling invisible threads connecting the bodiless voices" (151). La Trobe, the artist and creator, has the ability to pull together the various threads of these detached voices and this is where, she believes, her power comes from. La Trobe is not merely "a twitcher of individual strings; she was one who seeths wandering bodies and floating voices in a cauldron, and makes rise up from its amorphous mass a re-created world" (153). She not only unifies the discordant voices of literary history (which she knows still contains disjunctive breaks and transitions), she also brings together for a brief but artificial moment the discordant voices of her audience. Once the audience is placed in front of the stage, each member turns from his meaningless chatter to see himself reflected in the language of the literary history presented to him.

The members of the audience, on the other hand, have no control over what happens in front of them. As Bartholomew states, "Our part . . . is to be the audience. And a very important part too" (58). To be a member of the audience is to act a part of the play—each member helps to create the text of which he is also a spectator. Considering the nature of literary history, what Woolf implies here is that the audience also participates in the creation of the history that it appears to view from the outside. The subjectivity of the viewer is dependent on the outside world for its definition and distinction; and the world, the play, and literary history in this case, are dependent on the viewer.

However, most members of the audience cannot tolerate the emptiness that confronts them when they are between acts. Mrs. Manresa wants to "go and help" (59) while Giles Oliver has to remind her, "No, no . . . [we] are the audience" (59). But for Giles the words, "We remain seated—We are the audience"(59) are disturbing. On this particular afternoon the words "ceased to lie flat in a sentence" (59). Words "rose, became menacing and shook their fists at you" (59). Giles finds being part of the audience like being "manacled to a rock" and being "forced passively to behold indescribable horror" (60). What he will ultimately see is a reflection of himself in the world that the play represents, and this is what he fears most.

Silence, the lack of communication and interaction, is difficult to confront, and the audience would rather look for something to do, whether cutting bread and butter or engaging in mindless chatter. It is repeated throughout the novel that the audience has nothing to do, and it is the act of doing something that prevents the individuals that compose it from looking at and thinking about themselves. Candish, a gardener, and a maid "were all bringing chairs—for the audience. There was nothing for the audience to do" (65). The audience "stared at the view, as if something might happen in one of those fields to relieve them of the intolerable burden of sitting silent, doing nothing, in company. Their minds and bodies were too close, yet not close enough" (65). The outer scene, the field before them, represents the loneliness, alienation, and isolation that they try to escape from within themselves.

This confrontation with silence is most poignantly realized in the pageant's parody of the eighteenth-century comedy of manners. In this parody, Flavinda and Valentine secretly meet, and Flavinda goes through a long monologue of self-doubt. When the two lovers finally meet, an anonymous voice from the audience exclaims, "All that fuss about nothing!" The audience laughs, the voices stop, but the "voice had seen; the voice had heard" (138) and La Trobe "glowed with glory" that the truth had been understood. The actors in the pageant begin to weave in and out between the trees singing, and slowly the song dies out. They stand in front of the audience and "the audience sat staring at the villagers, whose mouths were opened, but no sound came" (141). For Miss La Trobe it is this silence that is "death."[15]

For the audience, too, the villagers' silence is self-annihilation, for behind the stage are empty fields that the audience needs to be buffered from. But before the illusion of the stage completely peters out, buried under the actors' silence, the "cows take up the burden" (140). The cows' bellows become the "primeval voice sounding loud in the ear of the present moment" (140), and their cries "annihilated the gap; bridged the distance; filled the emptiness and continued the emotion" (141). The fields that in fact show the audience its own isolation become the thing that prevents it. The outer world of the fields and cows becomes the inner world of the audience, and they help to continue the emotional response that the play had begun. As soon as the cows stop, however, the audience is once again confronted with the nothingness before them, and they "lowered their heads and read their programmes" (141) making sure they had something to occupy their wandering minds.

What takes place "between the acts" is a lack of communication. Only when the audience is in front of the text of the play is its thought reflected in a dialogical and interdependent relationship. It is only through language, and with the language of others, that the characters of the novel come to understand themselves. The effect of the outer world of language on the inner world of thought is reflected in the audience's response to what goes on before them. Besides the repetition of the phrase "We are dispersed" in Isa's mind, there are other characters, such as Mrs. Lynn Jones, who find themselves thinking about their lives in terms presented by the play. It is the literary history that helps Mrs. Jones to define herself in terms of her past.

During the Victorian section of the pageant the gramophone plays, "Home, Sweet Home." This song exemplifies the values that the Victorian age prefers, and these values cause Mrs. Jones to think about her mother, father, and their Victorian home. She says out loud, "it was beautiful," and with those words she is referring, not to the play, but "Home," the "lamplit room; the ruby curtains; and Papa reading aloud" (173). Etty Springett responds differently, and sees the play as "cheap and nasty." But Mrs. Jones still sees her home, and she begins to question why it no longer exists the way it did.

> Was there . . . something . . . perhaps "unhygienic" about the
> home? . . . Or why had it perished? Time went on and on like the
> hands of a kitchen clock. . . . The Home would have remained . . .
> Change had to come. . . . What she meant was, change had to
> come, unless things were perfect; in which case they resisted time.
> (174)

The play enters into Mrs. Jones's consciousness, causing her to think about her past, to be aware that things are not the same, and to question the nature of change. The evolution of these thoughts is a function of the pageant and its presentation of history; her subjective thoughts are a part of the objective world. It is through the objective world that Mrs. Jones comes to know herself and what is important to her.

The movement of Miss La Trobe's play through literary history culminates in the "present time," and it is at this moment that the audience is most disturbed about its implication in the meaning of the events. In the final act the audience sits while "[n]othing whatever appeared on the stage" (176). As they stare at the empty stage they feel trapped within their isolation, "They were all caught and caged; prisoners; watching a spectacle. Nothing happened" (176). They read in their programs that it is the "Present Time. Ourselves." No one knows what it means as they stare at the empty fields and listen to the gramophone tick time away.

With the lack of anything on stage, the audience does not know what to do, what to think, what its purpose is, and they find themselves almost unable to tolerate the extreme sense of detachment: "All their nerves were on edge. They sat exposed. The machine ticked. . . . They were neither one thing nor the other; neither Victorians nor themselves. They were suspended, without being, in limbo" (178). There is no text in front of them, no literary history, to help construct their identities, to give them thought and meaning. Isa begins to repeat the lines of a nursery rhyme, "Four and twenty blackbirds, strung upon a string" (178), while others reread their programs, "The Present Time. Ourselves. . . . Ourselves. . . They returned to the programme" (178). And so they asked, "But what could she know about ourselves?" (178). They ask what La Trobe could know about them, when in fact they know nothing about themselves without her.

La Trobe's dependency on her audience for her meaning also climaxes at this point in the play. La Trobe wants to "expose them, as it were, to douche them, with present-time reality" (179). But she realizes that this is too much for them, and her resentment toward them begins to emerge: "Audiences were the devil. O to write a play without an audience. Every second they were slipping the noose. Her little game had gone wrong. . . . This is death, death, death, she noted in the margin of her mind; when illusion fails" (180). La Trobe resents her dependency on the audience to create the meaning of her play. When the illusion she creates is not understood the way she intends it, it is just as if she hadn't created it at all. For her, there is no audience or conversation without their understanding, and without it there is no identity, and this brings death itself.

The scene shifts as rain suddenly begins to fall and La Trobe in her gratitude turns on the music, the simple tune of the nursery rhyme that runs in Isa's head. Woolf describes this music as "the other voice speaking, the voice that was no one's voice. . . . the voice that wept for human pain unending" (181). This voice both speaks to, and is the voice of, the audience. It enters to begin the dialogue and to create the meaning between the silence of the open fields, the emptiness of the stage, the rain that becomes tears, and the isolation of individuals in the audience. Only in relation to each other do these things gain their significance. The audience's attention is drawn to a scene that they take to be the meaning of the play and the history the play represents—"Civilization . . . in ruins; rebuilt . . . by human effort" (181).

But as the audience begins to be comforted by this scene, with its clear and lucid meaning, the music abruptly changes and they are thrown back into confusion. The type of music being played is unclear, it is something "half known, half not" (182). The tune "changed; snapped; broke; jagged," it is a "cackle, a cacophony" (183) and it foreshadows the disparity that is to follow. The children come out, described as "Imps-elves-demons," holding objects that reflect the images of the audience.

> Out they leapt, jerked, skipped. . . . Now old Bart . . . he was caught. Now Manresa. Here a nose . . . There a skirt . . . Then trousers only. . . . Ourselves? But that's cruel. To snap us as we are. . . . And only, too, in parts. . . . That's what's distorting and upsetting and utterly unfair. (184)

The literary history in which they are participating is a reflection of themselves; what each sees is fragmented and disparate, and they only see parts of themselves or parts of others. Their identities are distorted and unrecognizable, and this is difficult for them to accept, "all evaded and shaded themselves" (186). But it could not be otherwise, for identity is only fully known in relation to others and the world, and what is found without that relationship are parts and fragments. Like the cracked mirror in *To the Lighthouse*, what is outside is always broken and distorted. For the viewer to know that he is not whole without others to complete him, and to realize that identity is always split, is unbearable. It is better that the present moment not exist at all, and that we understand ourselves purely through history.

Amidst the chaos and confusion "a voice asserted itself," "[w]hose voice it was no one knew." It came from the bushes with "anonymous, loud-speaking affirmation" (186). The voice explains and describes the audience to itself, showing the differences between individuals and their hypocrisies. The anonymous voice uses a musical analogy to illustrate how the individuals in the audience are both separated from themselves and yet unified, different yet the same.

> The tune began; the first note meant a second; the second a third. Then down beneath a force was born in opposition; then another. On different levels they diverged. On different levels ourselves went forward; flower gathering some on the surface; others descending to wrestle with the meaning; but all comprehending; all enlisted. (189)

Underneath the order and sequence there is divergence and opposition. The divergence occurs on different levels, even within the individual, while some elements remain on the surface, taking obvious and literal meaning from things, other elements go for depth, investigating a meaning that is not quite as explicit. Each individual understands what he can, but only as a group, with all the various and disparate elements, can they comprehend the meaning of the whole—only in their disparity do they constitute a unity.

Reverend G. W. Streatfield is "one of the audience," one of the whole who is alike but different. He asks the audience as he asks himself, "what meaning, or message, this pageant was meant to convey?" (191) He admits that he is "puzzled" but proceeds to give his interpretation. The Reverend sees that "it was indicated that we are members one of another. Each is part of the whole. . . . We act different parts; but are the same" (192). He caught himself "too reflected, as it happened in my own mirror" and sees that they are all "scraps, orts and fragments! Surely, we should unite?" (192). The play ends with the gramophone gurgling, "Unity—Disparity" and then it ceases. And so it is that none "speaks with a single voice," a voice that is "free from old vibrations" (156). The voice of each person is the voice of the others, and every voice is the product of the voices that come before, the voices and vibrations of history. The closing of the novel does not represent a sense of beginning again, as many critics would argue. Instead, it reflects the reverberation of voices, the play behind the play, for, as La Trobe views it, "another play always lay behind the play she had just written" (63). The interaction between the language of subjective consciousness and the language of the other never ends.

Between the Acts presents the "orts and fragments" of which we, as Woolf's audience, are composed, our disparate and dispersed nature, and our utter dependence on the voice of the other to find our own. The narratives of our lives created through the artificial boundaries that Bernard discusses in *The Waves* are a function of the stories that are told about us, in the dramatic text of the world. Our voices, like the voices of *Three Guineas*, are not just dialogues, but echoes of the dialogues that we enter into.

Woolf's texts echo those of Leslie Stephen and Samuel Johnson. She is their reader, interpreter and audience. We find these echoes in the voices of her narratives, all of which contribute to the literary entity we call Virginia Woolf. We must model ourselves on her by recognizing that who we are as readers is always a function of what we have read, that as audience we are multiple and polyphonic, and as writers we contain infinite voices that are dependent on the world of readers and auditors for their form and meaning. Literary history is always a narrative of identity, and the kinds and numbers of histories are as varied as the voices of which we are composed. In this sense our voices continue to echo and repeat, always the same yet different, within the minds and texts of others.

The Conclusion, in which
Nothing is Concluded
—JOHNSON, "RASSELAS"

We live in a world where
nothing is concluded
—WOOLF, "ANON"

In *Virginia Woolf and Postmodernism*, Pamela L. Caughie dates the break in Woolf criticism as in or about December 1985. In that year Toril Moi's *Sexual/Textual Politics* was published, and Moi showed that Woolf criticism up to that moment had been determined by the realist aesthetics that modernism defined itself against. Moi called for a deconstructive reading of Woolf that would help us to understand both the feminist politics and modernist aesthetics in her work. Caughie points out that Moi's analysis endorses yet another kind of opposition, that between two schools of feminist thought—the American and the French. What Caughie states is needed in Woolf criticism is "a perspective that can free Woolf's writings from the cage of modernism and the camps of feminism without denying these relations in her texts" (2).

This study of Johnson and Woolf has laid out a method for understanding the relation between perspectives—whether feminist, modernist, historical, or otherwise—within a writer's texts, by demonstrating Johnson's desire to represent multiple points of view and Woolf's subsequent development of an alternative to the omniscient narrative "I." Woolf's essays not only illustrate Johnson's influence on her thinking, but also articulate the beginning of her experimentation in the representation of subjectivity. The intersection of subjectivity with narrative has been the basis for under-standing much of the modernist canon. The works of Woolf, as well as Joyce, Faulkner, Richardson, Stein, and others, have been discussed in terms of their ability to represent the workings of the inner mind. However, as we have seen, the subjective self and the notion of a guiding conscious-ness are no longer easy assumptions. In Woolf's work we find that the inner self is contingent upon the outer world, and that the subjective voice is composed of objective voices. The "stream" of consciousness no longer flows from a stable origin.

A further implication of this study is found in the notion of "influence." Woolf's relation to Johnson, as it has been argued here, is one that both places her within a standard tradition and takes Johnson out of his estab-lished realm. This kind of influence study is not the exaltation of a particu-lar writer as a means of establishing some ultimate literary goal, some promised land of narrative. This second idea defines influence with the terms it argues against: it assumes influence entails the development of an idea from one writer to another. The study of influence is not the study of teleology, but the study of reading and writing strategies. We cannot deny that what we write is a function of everything we have read, and that our writing is a response, just as Caughie responds to Moi, to all those various perspectives that enter our linguistic world. Literary history is an act of self-definition, where what we read and interpret, the connections and lineages we create, are more a statement of who and where we *are* than a statement of where we come from. Stephen's reading of Johnson is a response to the theological debate of his own time, and is a means of defining his own posi-tion within literary and social history. Woolf's reading of Johnson is a response to Stephen and his Victorian preoccupations. In her quest for originality and identity in a historical continuum, she has reread the figu-rations of her father in a stronger way.

Woolf discusses the idea of influence in *A Room of One's Own* when she says we must "think back through our mothers," and when she argues for a female literary tradition. But even if the tradition Woolf argues for did exist, where women writers are exclusively influenced by their literary mothers, how can we assume that all women would think, feel, experience, and write from the same perspective? Feminist critics, American and French alike, have tried to isolate the feminine and female, whether biological or gender coded, from the masculine or male mode of reading, writing, and critical approach.

Because of the political agendas involved on both sides of the controversy, parts of Woolf's reading history have been ignored. Though Woolf argued for a female tradition, she was also influenced (in an antithetical sense) by texts written by male writers. Johnson's texts, not Johnson the man, gave Woolf reading and writing strategies that allowed her to develop narrative forms that many feminist critics have pounced on as purely feminine, and modernist critics have taken as purely psychological. That is, reading and writing are rhetorical acts, processes that are learned and practiced, modeled on the rhetoric we encounter in our linguistic realms. Johnson's texts contain the moral, didactic, logocentric, and humanistic criteria that feminists have claimed address a masculine experience, despite humanism's claim to represent universal experience. The humanist reading is Stephen's monologic reading. But Johnson's texts also contain the dialogic, fluid, unstable, social, and process-oriented criteria that have been considered feminine. The reading and writing strategies Woolf brings to, and takes from, Johnson (since reading itself is dialogic) are used by her to develop her female literary history and to articulate the lack of female voices with which women writers need to interact.

This study has shown that the strategies used in Woolf's prose are part of a conversation she has had with Johnson and Stephen. What also informs her conversation are the many other female and male writers she came into contact with. Though Woolf is, unfortunately, the only female writer to gain the same respect and attention as her male counterparts in the modernist tradition, it does not mean that feminist critics are correct in their abduction and appropriation of Woolf's life and experience to justify their aesthetic criteria. However, this may not be the fault of critics who, by nature of their work, are forced to create boundaries to make order, much in the same way Bernard in *The Waves* is forced to construct his narratives. Perhaps the problem is found in our concepts of tradition and the canon. As limits and boundaries are set in order to present a coherent and lucid literary history, critics are forced to exclude anything that creates a sense of chaos and instability. Tradition and the canon are not exclusionary, leaving out some works to justify the inclusion of others. What is needed in our notions of tradition and the canon is a dialogic element that allows for disparity within a given writer's oeuvre, as well as in the critic's own *reading history*. It is in these terms that we can answer Caughie's question as to how we are to free both modernism and feminism without denying their relation to Woolf's texts and to each other.

My conclusion to this study of Johnson and Woolf should not be considered the telos of my research; nor do I claim to realign the disparity in Woolf criticism by emphasizing Johnson's influence. I only wish to enter the greater conversation between Woolf, Johnson, Stephen, their critics, and my readers, and to give the same sense of openness Woolf gives at the end of *Between the Acts*: "Then the curtain rose. They spoke" (219).

NOTES

Notes to Introduction

1. Though there have been a number of articles and unpublished dissertations written on Woolf's critical essays, there are only a few full-length studies on the subject. The most significant of these are: Mark Goldman, *The Reader's Art: Virginia Woolf as Literary Critic* (The Hague: Mouton, 1976) and Vijay L. Sharma, *Virginia Woolf as Literary Critic: A Revaluation* (New Delhi: Arnold-Heinemann, 1977). Perry Meisel's *The Absent Father* (New Haven, Conn.: Yale University Press, 1977) deals with the essays insofar as they demonstrate the influence of Paterian language and vision in Woolf.

2. See Meisel, p.xi, where he points out the influence of Ruskin, Arnold, and Pater, to whom the rest of his study is devoted. Goldman also argues that Woolf's critical precepts are oriented in Pater, but it is a Pater "redefined." V. L. Sharma places Woolf in a tradition with Matthew Arnold, Henry James, E. M. Forster, and T. S. Eliot. Others see Woolf's critical tenets as linked to her association with Bloomsbury. The first to point this out was Wyndham Lewis in *Men Without Art* (London: Cassell, 1934), 145. J. K. Johnstone developed this thesis in detail in *The Bloomsbury Group* (New York: Farrar, Strauss and Co., 1954). Virginia Hyman sees Leslie Stephen's "rational moralism" as an influence on Woolf's essentially "conservative" criticism. See Hyman, "Late Victorian and Early Modern," *English Literature in Transition* 23(1980): 144-54.

3. By "dialogical style," I refer to what Mikhail Bakhtin describes as "a diversity of social speech types (sometimes even diversity of languages) and a diversity of individual voices, artistically organized." "Discourse in the Novel" in *The Dialogic Imagination,* ed. Michael Holquist (Austin: University of Texas Press, 1981), 262.

Notes to Chapter 1

1. The reading Stephen and his contemporaries helped to form is the basis for twentieth-century views of Johnson. Critics such as T. S. Eliot, F. R. Leavis, Wimsatt and Brooks, Wellek, Bate, and Hagstrum place Johnson within a neoclassical tradition, with its emphasis on an ordered and hierarchical nature, morality, and the didactic function of art. Though Leavis sees Johnson as "subversive of neo-classic authority" (84), he argues that Johnson's "very decided conventions of idiom and form engage comprehensive unanimities regarding morals, society, and civilization" (71). Johnson, for Leavis, is part of a "great positive tradition" (71). Wimsatt and Brooks, in "The Neo-Classic Universal: Samuel Johnson," acknowledge that Johnson's "anti-classic revolt erupts with some energy rather early in his critical career" (325), but they struggle to keep Johnson within that tradition. Wimsatt and Brooks find within classicism four antitheses: "realism vs. fantasy, history vs. fiction, particular vs. universal, real vs. ideal" (334), and that these antitheses are subsumed in the neoclassical tradition under the basic antithesis, "nature vs. art." In Johnson's thinking, we note how "some of these antitheses clustered" (334). For Rene Wellek, Johnson's "moralism and realism combine with a strong and empathetic exposition of many of the central neoclassical tenets, especially the basic rationalistic view of art, and with a trained and self-conscious taste which worked with remarkable sureness within the body of accessible literature" (84). Bate argues that Johnson's criticism "proceeds through the tradition of neo-classic theory that had grown up since the Renaissance; but he accepts it as a pivot on which to revolve rather than a frame to limit the horizon. The most obvious way is his expansion of neo-classic values" (218). Hagstrum's study investigates how the notions of experience, reason,

nature, pleasure, beauty, the sublime, and wit manifest themselves in Johnson's writing. He concludes that "Morality, Johnson would seem to tell us, is in some form inescapable; and that literature which does not choose to illustrate it and enforce it will in one way or another have to reckon with it" (176-77).

2. For a full discussion of this controversy and its implications for Stephen's social and literary commentary, see John W. Bicknell, "Leslie Stephen's *English Thought in the Eighteenth Century*: A Tract of the Times," *Victorian Studies* 6 (1962): 103-20.

3. Noel Annan points out that Leslie Stephen's *English Thought in the Eighteenth Century* (1876) is an attempt to "rescue the English empiricists, Locke, Berkeley, Hume, from Taine's contention that they were insignificant" (223). Hans Aarsleff also sees *English Thought* as "an attempt to straighten out the history of the Lockean tradition" (139). John W. Bicknell describes the issues with which Stephen was dealing, and how Stephen used his *English Thought* as a means to attack the religious orthodoxy of his own time. Stephen saw that the Deists—Middleton, Hume, Gibbon, Locke, and others—had "taken up arms in the battle" (112). Stephen was reading the eighteenth century in terms of his own, "taking sides, seeking out allies, and disposing of enemies" (116). There is also a second theme in Stephen's *English Thought*: "[H]is account of the rationalist advance among the elite and its failure to attract followers, that is, of its superficial success and essential failure" (119).

4. That Hume is Stephen's rationalist "hero" is noted by Annan. Annan, however, has taken this statement from John Hunt's review of *English Thought*, "Mr. Leslie Stephen on English Thought in the Eighteenth Century," *Contemporary Review* XXIX (1877). In this review Hunt calls Stephen a "dogmatic unbeliever." John W. Bicknell points out that Hunt's review was a function of the late Victorians' theological debate, and Hunt was an orthodox reviewer. Hunt also states that Bishop Butler was Stephen's "rock of offense." Bicknell again corrects this reading by stating that Stephen found no offense in Butler, who was a major common sense philosopher of the time. Stephen saw his role in the writing of his history as an interrogator of both sides of the issue, pointing out the fallacies in everyone's logic. Butler "of all people, gets special praise because, while theologically unsound, he faced the facts of suffering and evil and did not attempt to wish them away" (Bicknell 120).

5. Johnson's philosophy of knowledge bears a keen resemblance to the common sense school. Chester Chapin, in "Samuel Johnson and the Scottish Common Sense School," points out that Johnson made many comments about the skeptical philosophers and the importance of common sense before Reid or the other Scottish philosophers published their works. Chapin argues that though Johnson did not belong to any philosophical school, "with regard to the Berkeley-Hume extension of Lockean empiricism, Johnson is in the camp of the opposition" (64). Chapin further states that eighteenth-century empiricism takes "two sharply divergent paths," one which is dominated by the immaterialism of Berkeley and the skepticism of Hume, and the other of the common sense orientation, which sees experience as the test by which speculation must be tried, though never ending in the annihilation of truth per se. Chapin suggests that there are two readings of Locke, and it is these two readings that Stephen's *History* attempts to untangle.

6. Stephen, like Johnson, believes one should, "Stick to the facts, and laugh at fine phrases. Clear your mind of cant. Work and don't whine. Hold fast by the established order, and resist anarchy as you would resist the devil" (Annan 376).

7. Manfred Weidhorn, in "The Conversation of Common Sense," tells us that in Johnson's conversation Johnson played the devil's advocate. In his conversation, Johnson examines the "validity of the minority idea, forcing the majority to reexamine its premise and to either purify its own argument, or to be converted to the Truth if it lies elsewhere" (4). Johnson was often "adopting the other person's premise in order to destroy the whole argument" (5). The function of common sense here is to "make distinctions." It is to see "two things where before we had seen only one thing; or, seeing things in per-

spective, as part of a totality, rather than discreetly; or, seeing the significance, the unique qualities of things while dismissing the accidental, the specious" (6).

Notes to Chapter 2

1. Samuel Johnson's preoccupation with the activity of conversation was not particular to him, but was a concern of many philosophers and moralists during the eighteenth century. Herbert Davis, in "The Conversation of the Augustans," points out that conversation "was a subject which had received frequent attention during the seventeenth century from writers who had concerned themselves with the manners and behavior of the young prince or courtier or the gentlemen as well as from the moralists who addressed themselves to a wider audience on the proper government of the tongue" (181). There is a long history of the "rhetoric of conversation," beginning with Cicero's *De Officiis*, which served as a guidebook of ethics in the eighteenth century, through Castiglione's *Book of Courtier* and Montaigne's essay "Of the Art of Discoursing." This art came into fruition during the eighteenth century (Broadhead 462).

Jonathan Swift and Henry Fielding wrote important polemics on the art of conversation. A short discussion of each will help us to understand Johnson's intellectual environment. Swift is a typical representative of eighteenth-century views on conversation, and, in his "Hints toward an Essay on Conversation," Swift is not concerned with conversation as one of the arts of the courtier, or as an accomplishment for those in polite society. Instead, he sees conversation "as a human privilege common to all civilized societies" (Davis 183). Conversation became "a new way of salvation" (Davis 186) in which men should talk together everyday. If conversation was to be a means of agreeable communication between civilized men and women, "the language of conversation must be kept free from all pedantries, all technical jargon, and all fashionable affectations" (Davis 188). It is the lack of pretension in language "that is the secret of power; that simplicity and ease which comes of modesty and good sense at the same time avoids all obscurity and allows the full effect of all that is there to be perceived and felt" (Davis 188). Therefore, those involved in conversation "will be easy, because there is nothing that they will not understand" (Davis 188).

Fielding, in his "Essay on Conversation," writes a kind of courtesy book as a guide to everyday relations with others. H. K. Miller has placed Fielding's essay in the eighteenth-century milieu, and he explains that Fielding treats conversation in the broadest sense of the term. Fielding defines conversation as "that reciprocal Interchange of Ideas, by which Truth is examined, Things are, in a manner, *turned round*, and sifted, and all our Knowledge communicated to each other" (Fielding 364). As Miller points out, in a society that saw conversation as a pleasure of life, it is hardly surprising that the idea of conversation as social talk should be linked with the notion of social intercourse (166). Fielding begins with the Aristotelian premise that as "conversation is a branch of society, it follows, that it can be proper to none who is not in his nature social" (Fielding 365). Fielding's essay, however, deals with manners, and it discusses how to converse "with God, with themselves, and with one another" (365). He gives a system of rules for talking up and down the social scale in order to accommodate the dissonance of social voices. He sees the art of conversation as the "art of pleasing or doing good to one another" (367). This, for Fielding, is part of "good-breeding," "the art of pleasing, or contributing as much as possible to the ease and happiness of those with whom you converse" (368). Fielding was most concerned to establish a guide by which men could learn to make their interaction with other men more fulfilling rather than merely more refined. For Fielding, like Swift, there is morality in the reconciliation of social differences. Both writers are concerned with conversation as a form of social action that occurs with ease, where speakers take responsibility for what is said and the way their auditors respond to their discourse: Swift and Fielding see conversation as human behavior with a moral base.

It is not unusual that Johnson should be concerned with the nature of conversation—it takes on moral significance and is consistent with his "common-sense" view of the world. The belief that morality can be achieved through an exchange between social classes and communication of knowledge through a language that all can understand, reveals the source of Johnson's use of conversation and dialogue as a vehicle for articulating the moral responsibilities of writing and reading.

This is not to say that Johnson did not see conversation in terms of hierarchy. Glenn J. Broadhead analyzes Johnson's rhetoric of conversation by elucidating what Johnson called his "laws of conversation" (Johnson, *Rambler* V: 152). Besides illustrating how natural it is that the world of Johnson's essays should be full of personae and characters whose "vices, vanities and foibles are reflected specifically in conversational gaucheries and errors"(464), Broadhead argues that Johnson's laws derive from a blend of "Christian faith, Ciceronian ethics, and Lockean psychology" (465). In Johnson's conception, the "laws" involve two main norms: subordination and mutuality. There are several kinds of subordination: violation of the Ciceronian injunction to conform to the properties of one's social rank; the willful disregard of the natural limitations of man's faculties in which each man is restricted to provinces of knowledge and ability; and to conform, in familiar discourse, to the properties of one's age (467-68). There are two remedies to subordination. First is the established modes of ceremony and politeness, and the other is to "accept the fact that one's relations with other men must be governed by the limitations ordained by God" (468).

Mutuality, the other norm of Johnson's laws of conversation, is the "lateral interdependence of man and man" (470). Thus, conversers must share a "disposition to the same inquiry, and delight in the same discoveries" (Johnson, *Rambler* IV: 167). Mutuality is "a willingness to explore all possibilities for mutual pleasure"(Broadhead 472); it is not only a "general resemblance" among conversers, as Johnson says, but also "dissimilitude," *concordia discours,* the "suitable disagreement" that is "necessary to intellectual harmony" (qtd. in Broadhead 473). Familiar discourse becomes "the successive and polar states of contention and concord, variety and unity, pain and pleasure" (474). Finally, it must be stated that Johnson does not see conversation, as Swift does, as the "art of pleasing," but as an art of exchange, where pleasure is found in mutual inquiry. Here we see the emergence of a notion of conversation as process, where value is obtained through the dynamic relation between points of view.

2. For a list of studies of Johnson as a "conversationalist," see James L. Clifford and Donald J. Greene, *Samuel Johnson: A Survey and Bibliography of Critical Studies* (Minneapolis: University of Minnesota Press, 1970), 151-53.

3. Johnson's doubts of being able to find the origin of a word's meaning are hinted at in the "Plan," and he states that it "is necessary likewise to explain many words by their opposition to others; for contraries are best seen when they stand together" (26). But this awareness does not come to fruition until he has completed the project. E. L. McAdam and George Milne, in their introduction to *Johnson's Dictionary: A Modern Selection,* also argue that when Johnson began the dictionary he thought stability in language desirable. He adhered to what McAdam and Milne call the "cyclical theory of language, after the model of the gold-silver-bronze ages of Latin literature" (x). Johnson thought English should be loyal to Old English origins and avoid Latin, and he objected to the importation of French words. By the time he had finished the dictionary, however, he was clear in his own mind that "language was in a state of constant change" (x). Johnson learned that the meaning of language is not stable but in flux, constantly growing and changing; he saw that meaning and knowledge are created through process.

4. See Robert DeMaria's *Johnson's "Dictionary" and the Language of Learning* (Chapel Hill: University of North Carolina Press, 1986) for a more complete list of references to Locke in the *Dictionary.*

5. Locke's argument in Book III is aimed at the most widely held seventeenth-century view of the nature of language, the "Adamic language." Adamic language, also an epistemological doctrine, held that "languages . . . despite their multiplicity and seeming chaos, contain elements of the original perfect language created by Adam when he named the animals in his prelapsarian state" (Aarsleff 25). In Adamic doctrine, "the relation between sign and signified is not arbitrary; the linguistic sign is not double but unitary" (25). Adamic doctrine had a "nomenclature, that words did name species and essences," and believed that language is a "better avenue to the true knowledge of nature than the mere self help of man's deceiving senses and imperfect reason" (26).

   Locke's essay is not "a metaphysical treatise, not a 'recherche de la verite'." It does not seek to offer a "complete system of knowledge and truth, but to present a discussion of the ways knowledge may be obtained and secured. Its nature is essentially practical, and for that reason it pays much attention to the ways in which we wrongly come to believe we have certain knowledge when in fact we do not" (Aarsleff 54). The Essay is about "process, not about the still center and the possible" (55).

6. Hans Aarsleff, in From Locke to Saussure (Minneapolis: University of Minnesota Press, 1982), also argues that Locke's theory is "entirely functional" (28) and that Locke viewed language as a "social institution" (28).

7. John McLaverty argues that, though Johnson started his dictionary by attempting, in Johnson's words, to limit every idea by a definition "strictly logical," Johnson realized that ideas had more than one meaning. Instead, Johnson gave a historical, evolutionary explanation, versus definition, to the word. Thus, McLaverty points out, Locke's theory of knowledge as process becomes important to Johnson (377). Johnson creates meaning through difference; he shows us the definition of a word by placing all its possible connotations in dialogue with one another. What Johnson learned from Locke was not so much a philosophical system "as a general approach to problems of knowledge, an approach which was genetic, historical, and . . . social" (394).

8. In terms of Bakhtinian dialogics, a voice is not just "words or ideas strung together: it is a 'semantic position,' a point of view on the world, it is one personality orienting itself among personalities within a limited field. . . . How a voice sounds is a function of where it is and what it can 'see', its orientation is measured by the field of responses it evokes" (Emerson, Preface to PDP xxxvi).

9. Bakhtin has included in his notion of Menippea the "carnivalistic." The carnivalistic consists of the "[m]ulti-toned narration, the mixing of high and low, serious and comic . . . the mixing of prosaic and poetic speech, living dialects and jargons . . ." (Bakhtin, PDP 108).

10. Johnson's discourse contains what Bakhtin calls an "internal dialogicality" where "the diatribe is an internally dialogized rhetorical genre, usually structured in the form of a conversation with an absent interlocutor—and resulting in a dialogization of the very process of speech and thought" (Bakhtin, PDP 120).

11. Sheldon Sacks, in his Fiction and the Shape of Belief, defines the structure and genre of Rasselas as an "apologue." An apologue is "organized as a fictional example of the truth of a formuable statement or closely related set of such statements" (8). In its most prosaic form "the concept obviously illustrated in Rasselas is that earthly happiness does not exist" (49).

    Though Sacks acknowledges that Rasselas is not a "species of philosophical dialogue" (56), his analysis entails a monologic conception of knowledge. That is, the "formuable statement" that the fictional examples contribute to is a unified statement that is the product of a unified and singular consciousness, either the author's or the character's. This, according to Bakhtin, is a form of idealism (PDP 80). Idealism "knows only a single mode of cognitive interaction among consciousnesses: someone who knows and possesses the truth instructs someone who is ignorant of it and in error; that is, it is the interaction of a teacher and a pupil, which . . . can be only a pedagogical dialogue" (81).

Notes to Chapter 3

1. See Virginia Hyman, "The Metamorphosis of Leslie Stephen." *Virginia Woolf Quarterly* 2 (1974): 48-65.

2. Direct allusions to Johnson can be found in the following essays: "Their Passing Hour" (1905); "The Bluest of the Blue" (1906); "A Swan and Her Friends" (1907); "A Stranger in London" (1908); "A Friend of Johnson" (1909); "The Genius of Boswell" (1909); "Sheridan" (1909); "Sterne" (1909); "A Man with a View" (1916); "Creative Criticism" (1917); "Addison" (1919); "Patmore's Criticism" (1921); "Gothic Romance" (1921); "An Impression of Gissing" (1923); "How it Strikes a Contemporary" (1923); "Indiscretions" (1924); "Peggy" (1924); "How Should One Read a Book?" (1926); "Women and Fiction" (1929); "Dr. Burney's Evening Party" (1929); "The Essays of Augustine Birrell" (1930); "Great Men's Houses" (1932); "Congreve's Comedies" (1937); "The Art of Biography" (1939); "Mrs. Thrale" (1941); "Byron and Mr. Briggs" (1979). See Elizabeth Steele, *Virginia Woolf's Sources and Allusions: A Guide to the Essays* (New York: Garland Publishing, 1983).

3. Review of *The Life of Johnson*. Vol. 2, May 22, 1925, pp. 103-109. Berg Collection, New York Public Library.

4. Katherine C. Hill's unpublished dissertation, "Virginia Woolf and Leslie Stephen: A Study in Mentoring and Literary Criticism" (Columbia University, 1979), defines Woolf's psychological "identification" with Stephen and describes his training of Woolf as a literary critic. Hill traces Stephen's theory of literary history in Woolf's critical work. See also Louise DeSalvo, James Hafley, Herbert Marder and Brenda Silver.

5. There have been a number of studies concerning Stephen's influence on Woolf. I would like to sketch out, though a bit unwieldy for a note, the trends of these influence studies so that we may see how the notion of "influence" has been understood in Woolf scholarship. The studies are psychological, stressing Stephen's oppressive influence as contributing to Woolf's views on women, sexuality, and woman's role in society; or the studies concentrate on Stephen's intellectual influence on Woolf's development as a writer and thinker. One of the earliest essays, "Leslie Stephen's Daughter" (1953), by Hilda Ridley, sets the terms for following discussions of the Stephen/Woolf relationship. According to Ridley, Woolf perceives her father as the rational, moral Victorian, and her mother, Julia Duckworth Stephen, as the creative, social, "angel in the house." According to Ridley, Virginia admires the qualities of her mother and resents those of her father. These attitudes are represented in her portrayal of her parents in *To the Lighthouse*.

Herbert Marder, whose work *Feminism and Art: A Study of Virginia Woolf* (Chicago: University of Chicago Press, 1968) began the long-term debate on Woolf's feminism, develops Ridley's thesis; like Ridley, Marder sees Leslie Stephen as a Victorian who emphasized "(masculine) rational faculties to the exclusion of the (feminine) faculties of intuition" (3). Woolf's feminism "grew out of a desire for wholeness and harmony" (4). The feminist attitudes found in Woolf's work, as it develops later in her life, are related to "class and family background—particularly the influence of her father and his ideas" (10).

The class and family background to which Marder refer are described by Noel Annan in "The Intellectual Aristocracy." Annan describes Stephen's influence on Woolf by tracing the growth of a new academic and intellectual class in early nineteenth-century England, their propensity to intermarry, and their position in the Victorian class structure. Woolf was born into the intellectually privileged aristocracy that Annan describes, as were her intimates of Bloomsbury.

More recent work concerning Stephen's influence on Woolf describes the psychological implications of her training and education at home. Louise DeSalvo's "1897: Virginia Woolf at Fifteen," reveals the psychological mechanisms found in Woolf's intellectual development. DeSalvo points out that in 1897, when Woolf was recovering from her mother's death, she was given the medical treatment of solitude and isolation.

Deprived of the company of peers "Woolf had nothing against which to judge herself other than the measure of her family" (82). To replace this lack of social interaction, Woolf defined herself through her reading: "She carved out an identity for herself, as a historian in the making. . . . In 1897 Leslie Stephen continued to encourage his daughter to become a historian or a biographer" (87). History and biography gave her structure and a sense of purpose, and this sense of identity can be found throughout her work.

Other studies, less psychological, emphasize the intellectual influence of Stephen on Woolf and, like DeSalvo, see it in terms of history and biography. The most substantial and penetrating work on Stephen's intellectual influence is found in S. P. Rosenbaum's "An Educated Man's Daughter: Leslie Stephen, Virginia Woolf, and the Bloomsbury Group." As Rosenbaum rightly points out, criticism has paid little attention to Woolf's "literary and intellectual heritage." Feminist criticism, for the most part, "shuns the principal traditions of literature and ideas in which she developed because they were masculine . . . to diminish her achievement by treating her work as if literary and intellectual history were irrelevant to it" (35). But, we can look at Woolf as a member of Bloomsbury, and Stephen was an intellectual father to the entire group. He was "significant for Bloomsbury and his daughter as a Victorian philosopher and historian of ideas, as a literary historian and critic, and—perhaps most important—as a biographer" (36). For Rosenbaum, "Virginia Woolf's was a prose inheritance" (53). Stephen's "lucid, moral, rational, common sensical conception of literature was a logically necessary though emotionally insufficient precursor of her own" (53).

Katherine C. Hill also discusses Stephen's literary and intellectual influence on Woolf's conception of history and biography. As others point out, Hill reminds us of Stephen's role as Woolf's mentor: "[He] tutored Virginia extensively in biography as well as history, and this education, stemming as it did from Stephen's beliefs about the interrelations of biography, history, and literature, was crucial in shaping her own approach to literary criticism and her theorizing about the development of literary genres" (353). Hill sees the most provocative trace of Stephen's teaching in the "similarity between the father's and daughter's theorizing on how literary genres develop and evolve" (355). Woolf received his "conceptions of social and literary process" (355). This is found in their shared belief in the relationship between class structure and literary genre.

Virginia Hyman, twenty years after Ridley's article, discusses the representation of Stephen in *To the Lighthouse*. Hyman gives a more complex reading to the novel by pointing out that "Stephen's ideas and values are not nearly as one-dimensional as Mr. Ramsay's, and that, rather than being 'contained' in Mr. Ramsay, [the ideas] pervade the novel. What we will see is that, far from exorcising her father's 'influence' by caricaturing Mr. Ramsay, Virginia Woolf has dealt with his ideas and values in a remarkably complex and skillful way" (48). Hyman says it is as if "the novelist had 'split' Stephen's attitudes and values, assigning the rational, linear, analytic and objective ones to Mr. Ramsay, and the sympathetic, intuitive, and synthesizing ones to Mrs. Ramsay" (59): both characters represent Leslie Stephen. In a later article, Hyman argues Stephen's influence on Woolf is a conservative one. What she inherited from Stephen, according to Hyman, is a sense of morality when judging a piece of literature. Woolf is "concerned with its connection to the life of the writer. She often shares Stephen's specific enthusiasm and prejudices, and often gives the same reasons" (149). Woolf's "criticism exemplifies her conscious attempt to preserve the best traditions of English fiction by reasserting the critical values that she had inherited from her father" (152).

It is not my purpose to dispute the verity of the preceding studies, only to demonstrate the trends that Woolf scholarship has followed when discussing Stephen's influence on Woolf: biographical, psychological, intellectual, and literary. The present study utilizes the concept of "influence" as it is defined by Harold Bloom, and thereby forces us to look at Stephen's "influence" on Woolf in a new way.

6. Bate argues that the Johnson's criticism "proceeds through the tradition of the neoclassic theory that had grown up since the Renaissance; but he accepts it as a pivot on which to revolve rather than a frame to limit the horizon. The most obvious way is his expansion of neoclassic values" (218). Johnson allows classical values to become more subtle; "the ideal of decorum is made kinetic and more ample" (219).

7. W. R. Keast describes Johnson's notion of "nature" as the "link between author and reader." For Johnson, "nature is not an ontological, but a psychological, concept: it is defined, that is, not in terms of properties independent of the mind but in terms of its capacity to produce certain responses in men" (399). The audience to which the literary process is directed is the Common Reader. The importance of the reader in Johnson's scheme lies in the fact that Johnson is seeking "a stable basis in nature on which to rest critical inquiry and judgement: the audience is the only fixed element in the process" (402).

8. In discussing Woolf's critical essays, Pamela Caughie points out that Woolf develops a comparative approach, "pitting different narratives against each other, looking at the differences within as well as among phases, and considering the kinds of beliefs and assumptions we agree to in different novels" (175).

9. Andrew McNeillie also views conversation as a characteristic element in Woolf's essays, though he does not comment on how she incorporates this into the structure of her essays. In the introduction to *The Common Reader: First Series* he writes: "For her part she was content to write, as a reviewer, essays that share something of the immediacy, the flashing brilliance and unscholarliness of conversation in which (invariably unidentified) quotations are capped and a dinner-table intimacy is assumed. She believed in the momentary insight, the sudden recognition, a property of conversation (and of poetry)" (xii).

10. Jeanne Dubino argues that the conversational element in Woolf's criticism is a function of the "tea-table" society of which she was a part. The influence of this etiquette, which determines much of the tone and style of Woolf's essays, finds its expression during Johnson's time as well.

Notes to Chapter 4

1. Gary Saul Morson and Caryl Emerson use the term "active understanding" to describe the notion of dialogue as it is intended by Mikhail Bakhtin. See *Mikhail Bakhtin: Creation of a Prosaics* (Stanford: Stanford University Press, 1990), 128-29.

2. This differs from contemporary reader-response theory, which concerns itself with how readers interpret texts *after* they are made. For further discussion see Morson and Emerson (129).

3. Alex Zwerdling has commented that Woolf's work carries on a "kind of dialogue with other voices in her culture" (36) and that her work reflects "her complex sense of how historical forces and societal institutions influence the behavior of the people she describes" (3). Though Zwerdling is correct in his assessment, he does not pursue the link between public and private worlds and Woolf's style and technique. Instead, he describes how particular historical events and traditions inform and determine the content of her work. That is, it is not the dynamic between inner and outer worlds that he analyzes, but how the public sphere is represented in the private.

4. Makiko Minow-Pinkney views Woolf's concept of androgyny as a method by which Woolf can account for both the internal world of the female subject and her existence in the external, dominant, male ideology of what Lacan calls the symbolic order. Woman is "androgynous because of this internal 'split' in her consciousness" (10). This redefinition of the essentialist version of androgyny marks the "female" by its relation to, and entrance in, language. The role of language in identity formation is what is at issue here.

5. For further discussion of Woolf as a writer of history see: Katherine C. Hill, "Virginia Woolf and Leslie Stephen: History and Literary Revolution," *PMLA* 96 (1981): 351-62; Virginia R.

Hyman, "Late Victorian and Early Modern: Continuities in the Criticism of Leslie Stephen and Virginia Woolf," *English Literature in Transition* 23 (1980): 144-54; Brenda R. Silver, "Virginia Woolf and the Elizabethans" (Doctoral dissertation, Harvard University, 1973)

6. For example, Mitchell Leaska reads *Mrs. Dalloway* as a novel about marriage and heterosexuality by contrasting Clarissa's views and relationships to her alter ego, Septimus Smith (113-15). Zwerdling, on the other hand, approaches the novel with a much broader agenda, arguing that the novel fulfills Woolf's desire to criticize the social system by capturing "a moment in which the domination of the ideal of rigid self-control began to seem oppressive rather than admirable" (143).

7. Susan Dick does not view this narrative strategy, at least in Woolf, as an attempt to replicate consciousness, but rather as an "aspect of consciousness" (177). Her concern is with the role of memory in what she terms the "tunnelling process." But this analysis also assumes that the subject in whom the memories have their origins is unified. Even memory—that is, what we choose to remember—is a function of the world outside of ourselves.

8. For Lacan, the subject's identity is found in the "symbolic." Entrance into the symbolic occurs during the "mirror stage," where the unformed self finds definition through images that are other than itself. Lacan explains the function of the mirror stage in relation to the symbolic and the role of language in completing identity: "The human being sees his form materialized, whole, the mirage of himself, outside of himself. . . . What the subject, the one who exists, sees in the mirror is an image, whether sharp or broken up, lacking in consistency, incomplete. . . . Now let us postulate that the inclination of the plane mirror is governed by the voice of the other. This doesn't happen at the level of the mirror-stage, but it happens subsequently through our overall relation with others—the symbolic relation. . . . What is the symbolic connection? . . . it is the fact that socially we define ourselves with the law as go-between. It is through the exchange of symbols that we locate our different selves in relation to one another" (140).

9. The self-reflexive quality of Woolf's narrative has been addressed by only a few of her readers. Pamela Caughie writes that *To the Lighthouse* is a novel about the narrative function of the artist. Woolf created "her first artist figure to tell the story of her own artwork as well as the story in which her artwork figures" (33). Anne Herrmann claims the novel "constructs its literary heroine as a dialogized subject by representing her in terms of the female artist's relation to her subject: Lily Briscoe paints Mrs. Ramsay, who is the creator of atmosphere rather than art" (62-63). Woolf, in turn, creates Lily. Gayatri Spivak reads the novel as the story of "Mr. Ramsay (philosopher-theorist) and Lily (artist-practioner) around Mrs. Ramsay (text)" (310). This reading, like the others, illustrates how the novel is about its own creation and interpretation.

10. Every topic we speak about is determined by other utterances on that topic. In fact, the topic is overdetermined by voices. Dialogue is not to be conceptualized as a model of a script, where one speech simply follows another; the "complexities created by the already-spoken-about quality of the word, and by the listener's active understanding, create an *internal dialogism* of the word" (Morson and Emerson 138).

11. The concept of "inner speech" is borrowed from L. S. Vygotskii, *Thought and Language* (Cambridge: M.I.T. Press, 1962). As Vygotskii explains, the "plane of inner speech lies beyond the semantic plane" (130). Inner speech is not merely verbal memory, speech minus sound, or the whole interior aspect of any speech activity. Inner speech is "speech for oneself; external speech is for others. . . . The latter is the turning of thought into words, its materialization and objectification. With inner speech, the process is reversed: speech turns into inward thought" (131). Inner speech is a process and a relationship based on an interaction with the outside world: "Inner speech is something new brought in from the outside along with socialization" (136).

Notes to Chapter 5

1. J. W. Graham discusses this search for perspectives by comparing the use of first person narration in the first draft to Bernard's final monologue. Bernard's (internal) monologue, according to Graham, allowed Woolf to organize the various perspectives and this is what she had been searching for all along. I would argue that Bernard's monologue does not represent the unity of the structure, but the actual disparity of it. Bernard defines himself as fragmented, composed of those he comes into contact with, and the narrative of the novel as a whole is composed of this same kind of fragmentation.

2. See Avrom Fleishman on soliloquy (152), Patricia Laurence on musical form (192-204), Ralph Freedman on poetry and lyric form (185-270), and Mary Ann Caws, who argues that Woolf's preoccupation in this novel is "always with perception, whose crucial processes are a deep fascination with the various, six-sided sight as opposed to the single one" (249).

3. Though Edward Bishop agrees that the narrative is "never truly dramatic" he insists that we receive each character's experience through "some narrating consciousness" (98). It is the lack of an omniscient or guiding narration that Woolf strives for.

4. Jean Guiguet discusses the meaning and function of the six "characters" in the novel and Woolf's relation to them. The characters are not "detached from one another as their separate names and bodies and apparent destinies might suggest. And this effacement of their individuality, of the differences between them, only increases the temptation, for the author to mingle with them, to become part of them. . . . these are not six voices in search of characters, but a single being in search of voices" (284-85).

5. I refer to the model of communication developed by Roman Jakobson, where any speech event is understood as consisting of six constituent factors: addresser, addressee, context, message, contact, and code.

context
message
addresser————————————————————————addressee
contact
code

(Jakobson 353)

The Waves, however, does not follow this model. There is no "addressee" and we are unaware of the "context" of the message.

6. Rhoda's psychotic state has been described as Woolf's representation of female hysteria, and in this way Woolf inscribes silence onto the female body. Rhoda's identity is therefore defined as lack or negativity (Laurence 130-31). She cannot construct a voice for herself because she is separated from the world around her.

7. For Pater, all art aspires to the condition of music where form and content are one: "It is the art of music which most completely realizes this artistic ideal, this perfect identification of form and matter. In its ideal, consummate moments, the end is not distinct from the means, the form from the matter, the subject from the expression; they inhere in and completely saturate each other; and to it, therefore, to the condition of its perfect moments, all the arts may be supposed constantly to tend and aspire" (57).

8. Mark Hussey has called the novel an "aesthetic failure" because it represents "anti-reading." That is, "it does not allow for the participation of the reader, but continually dictates through a highly self-conscious structure" (86). It is Hussey's phenomonological orientation that prevents him from viewing the reader's self-consciousness as a function of his participation with the text.

9. Jane Marcus argues that Woolf defined herself in Three Guineas as an "outsider, a feminist, socialist, artist and worker" (284) in order to critique the relationship between fascism and patriarchy, while Alex Zwerdling sees the essay as a means to vent Woolf's twin needs: "anger about the subjection of women and to conciliate the male audience she could never entirely ignore" (243). Pamela Caughie and Anne Herrmann, on the other hand, address the narrative structure and how that structure undermines a

unified and central authority. The rhetoric of *Three Guineas* allowed Woolf "to remain uncommitted to any one position, thereby enabling her to investigate the complexities of tyranny" (Caughie 116). One kind of rhetoric used to investigate these complexities is the way in which "the multiplicity of interlocutors and the self-effacement of the locutor undermine the subjective nature of the epistle by rewriting intersubjectivity as anonymity" (Herrmann 52). I would argue that the use of first person is broken down into a dialogic subjectivity that could be understood as self-effacement or anonymity, but nevertheless deconstructs the very notion of authority it assumes to critique.

10. Northrop Frye defines Menippean satire as a structural principle or attitude. In what he calls the "short form" of Menippean satire, there is usually dialogue or colloquy, in which the dramatic interest is in a conflict of ideas rather than character. Woolf's essay is Menippean if she is understood to have the following objective in mind: "The Menippean satirist, dealing with intellectual themes and attitudes, shows his exuberance in intellectual ways, by piling up an enormous mass of erudition about his theme or in overwhelming his pedantic targets with an avalanche of their own jargon" (311). What appear to be digressions are "scholarly distillations of Menippean forms." It is an "anatomy" or dissection or analysis, and we might adopt the term "anatomy" to replace what is a misleading term for contemporary readers, "Menippean satire" (311-12).

11. In the introductory essay to *Reading at Random*, which Woolf was working on concurrently with *Between the Acts*, she explains the relationship between creator and audience: "The poet is no longer a nameless wandering voice, but attached to his audience. tethered [sic] to one spot and played upon by outside influences" ("Anon" 390).

12. It is the question of form that has preoccupied many critics of the novel. The debate concerns whether the narrative is unified or fragmented. Mark Hussey views *Between the Acts* as a "fully integrated work of art in which the play between individual consciousness and cultural memory is the substance of the book" (131). Nora Eisenberg also hopes to unify both the form and content of the novel by focusing on Woolf's use of music and song to expose "the limitations of language as such and the virtues of different communicative forms that might better pull life together" (255). In contrast, Alex Zwerdling and Patricia Laurence concentrate on the element of fragmentation in the novel. The pageant is an attempt "to trace the pervasive sense of fragmentation and isolation in the modern world to its historical roots" (Zwerdling 317). In *Between the Acts* we hear "a different kind of music," one in which the "harmony of Nature and human voices is shattered in war and the disjunctions of interruption are heard" (Laurence 180).

13. Another approach to the dialogic form is offered by Anne Herrmann, who believes *Between the Acts* can be read as a fiction that can "rewrite the dialogic relation between literature and history as historical fiction" (118).

14. According to Patricia Maika, the components of *Between the Acts* are reminiscent of Greek theater. There is the emphasis on the fictional artist, Miss La Trobe, whose mind is porous enough to absorb the emotions and logic of civilization while having the language to give them shape and meaning for the audience. We also find the miniature world, Pointz Hall, which is suspended in time and yet recalls the ancient theater of Dionysos in Athens. Finally, there is the suggestion of a kind of participatory reading, merging the "imagination and insight" with the reader's own (5). Melba Cuddy-Keane stresses the relationship between La Trobe and her audience. By transforming all voices into a chorus, Woolf "subverts the habitual dominance of the leader figure and introduces a new concept of community in which the insider-outsider dichotomy is erased and the bond of common identity is rewritten as a unifying participation in common action" (275).

15. Woolf describes the role of silence in her essay "Anon." The silence that an audience feels is "one of the deep gulfs that lies between us and the play" (395). Like the Elizabethan audience, La Trobe's audience, "drawn though it is by an irresistible attraction to the play, is silent" (395). Again like the Elizabethan audience, for La Trobe's audience "the expressive power of words after their long inadequacy must have been overwhelming" (395).

WORKS CITED

PRIMARY WORKS
SAMUEL JOHNSON

Johnson, Samuel. *The Idler and The Adventurer.* Edited by Bate, Bullitt, and Powell. New Haven and London: Yale University Press, 1963. Vol. 2 of *The Yale Edition of the Works of Samuel Johnson.* 15 vols.

————. *Lives of the English Poets.* Edited by George Birkbeck Hill. 3 vols. Oxford: Clarendon Press, 1905.

————. *Plan of a Dictionary.* Edited by R. C. Alston. Menston, England: The Scolar Press, 1970.

————. *The Rambler.* Edited by W. J. Bate and Albrecht B. Strauss. New Haven and London: Yale University Press, 1969. Vols. 3-5 of *The Yale Edition of the Works of Samuel Johnson.* 15 vols.

————. *Rasselas and Other Tales.* Edited by Gwin J. Kolb. New Haven and London: Yale University Press, 1990. Vol. 6 of *The Yale Edition of the Works of Samuel Johnson.* 15 vols.

————. Preface. *The Works of William Shakespeare.* Edited Arthur Sherbo. New Haven and London: Yale University Press, 1968. Vol. 7 of *The Yale Edition of the Works of Samuel Johnson.* 15 vols.

LESLIE STEPHEN

Stephen, Leslie. *English Literature and Society in the Eighteenth Century.* New York: G.P. Putnam's Sons, 1904.

————. *Essays on Freethinking and Plainspeaking.* New York and London: G.P. Putnam's Sons, 1908.

————. *History of English Thought in the Eighteenth Century.* 2d ed. 2 vols. New York: G.P. Putnam's Sons, 1927.

————. *Hours in a Library.* 2d ed. 4 vols. New York: G.P. Putnam's Sons, 1907.

————. "Johnsoniana." In *Studies of a Biographer.* 4 vols. London: Duckworth and Co.; New York: G.P. Putnam's Sons, 1899-1902.

————. *Men, Books, and Mountains.* Edited by S.O.A. Ullman. London: Hogarth Press, 1956.

————. *Samuel Johnson.* London and New York: Macmillan, 1900.

VIRGINIA WOOLF

Woolf, Virginia. *Between the Acts.* New York: Harcourt, 1941.

————. "The Bluest of the Blue." In *The Essays of Virginia Woolf.* vol. 1. Edited by Andrew McNeillie. New York: Harcourt, 1986.

————. "Addison." In *The Common Reader.* London: Hogarth; New York: Harcourt, 1925.

————. "Byron & Mr. Briggs." In *The Essays of Virginia Woolf.* vol. 2. Edited by Andrew McNeillie. New York: Harcourt, 1986.

————. "The Common Reader." In *The Common Reader.* London: Hogarth; New York: Harcourt, 1925.

————. "Congreve's Comedies." In *The Moment, and Other Essays.* Edited by Leonard Woolf. London: Hogarth, 1947; New York: Harcourt, 1948.

————. "A Friend of Johnson's." In *Granite and Rainbow: Essays.* Edited by Leonard Woolf. London: Hogarth; New York: Harcourt, 1958.

————. "Hours in a Library." In *Collected Essays.* vol. 2. Edited by Leonard Woolf. New York: Harcourt, 1967.

————. "How It Strikes a Contemporary." In *The Common Reader.* London: Hogarth; New York: Harcourt, 1925.

————. "How Should One Read a Book?" In *The Common Reader: Second Series*. London: Hogarth, 1932. Published as *The Second Common Reader*. New York: Harcourt, 1932.

————. "The Leaning Tower." In *The Moment and Other Essays*. New York: Harcourt, 1947.

————. "A Letter to a Young Poet." In *The Death of the Moth and Other Essays*. New York: Harcourt, 1942.

————. "A Man with a View." In *Contemporary Writers*. Compiled by Jean Guiguet. London: Hogarth, 1965. New York: Harcourt, 1966.

————. "Mr. Conrad: A Conversation." In *The Captain's Death Bed and Other Essays*. Edited by Leonard Woolf. London: Hogarth, 1947; New York: Harcourt, 1948.

————. "The Modern Essay." In *The Common Reader*. London: Hogarth; New York: Harcourt, 1925.

————. *Mrs. Dalloway*. London: Hogarth; New York: Harcourt, 1925.

————. "Patmore's Criticism." In *Books and Portraits*. Edited Mary Lyons. New York: Harcourt, 1977.

————. "The Patron and the Crocus." In *The Common Reader*. London: Hogarth; New York: Harcourt, 1925.

————. Review of *The Life of Johnson*. vol. 2, May 22, 1925, pp.103-109. Berg Collection, New York Public Library.

————. *A Room of One's Own*. New York: Harcourt, 1929.

————. "Their Passing Hour." In *The Essays of Virginia Woolf*. vol. 1. Edited by Andrew McNeillie. New York: Harcourt, 1986.

————. *Three Guineas*. London: Hogarth; New York: Harcourt, 1938.

————. *To the Lighthouse*. London: Hogarth; New York: Harcourt, 1927.

————. *The Waves*. London: Hogarth; New York: Harcourt, 1931.

————. *A Writer's Diary*. Edited by Leonard Woolf. New York: Harcourt, 1953.

SECONDARY WORKS
SAMUEL JOHNSON

Bate, W. J. *The Achievement of Samuel Johnson*. Chicago: University of Chicago Press, 1978.

Boswell, James. *The Life of Johnson*. Edited by R. W. Chapman. New York: Oxford University Press, 1983.

Broadhead, Glenn J. "Samuel Johnson and the Rhetoric of Conversation." *Studies in English Literature: 1500-1900* 20 (1980): 461-74.

Chapin, Chester. "Samuel Johnson and the Scottish Common Sense School." *Eighteenth Century* 20 (1979): 50-64.

Clifford, James L., and Donald J. Greene. *Samuel Johnson: A Survey and Bibliography of Critical Studies*. Minneapolis: University of Minnesota Press, 1970.

Damrosch, Leopold. *The Uses of Johnson's Criticism*. Charlottesville: University Press of Virginia, 1976.

Davis, Herbert. "The Conversation of the Augustans." In *The Seventeenth Century: Studies in the History of English Thought and Literature from Bacon to Pope*. Stanford: Stanford University Press, 1951.

De Maria, Robert, Jr. "The Theory of Language in Johnson's *Dictionary*." In *Johnson After Two Hundred Years*. Edited by Paul J. Korshin. Philadelphia: University of Pennsylvania Press, 1986.

Donner, H. W. "Dr. Johnson as a Literary Critic." In *Samuel Johnson: A Collection of Critical Essays*. Edited by Donald J. Greene. Englewood Cliffs, N.J.: Prentice-Hall, Inc., 1965.

Eliot, T. S. "Johnson as Critic and Poet." In *On Poetry and Poets*. London: Faber & Faber, 1957.

Fielding, Henry. "Essay on Conversation." In *Miscellaneous Writings*. vol. 1. New York: Croscup and Sterling Co., 1902.

Hagstrum, Jean H. *Samuel Johnson's Literary Criticism*. Chicago: University of Chicago Press, 1967.

Keast, William R. "The Theoretical Foundations of Johnson's Criticism." In *Critics and*

Criticism: Ancient and Modern. Edited by Ronald S. Crane. Chicago: University of Chicago Press, 1952.

Lipking, Lawrence. *The Ordering of the Arts in Eighteenth-Century England.* Princeton: Princeton University Press, 1961.

Locke, John. *An Essay Concerning Human Understanding.* Abridged and Edited by Raymond Wilburn. London: J. M. Dent and Sons; New York: E. P. Dutton, 1947.

McAdam, E. L., and George Milne. *Johnson's Dictionary: A Modern Selection.* New York: Pantheon Books, 1963.

McLaverty, James. "From Definition to Explanation: Locke's Influence on Johnson's Dictionary." In *Journal of the History of Ideas* 47.3 (1986): 377-394.

Miller, H. K. *Essays on Fielding's "Miscellanies": A Commentary on Volume One.* Princeton: Princeton University Press, 1961.

Sacks, Sheldon. *Fiction and the Shape of Belief.* Berkeley: University of California Press, 1963.

Swift, Jonathan. "Hints Toward an Essay on Conversation." In *The Prose Works of Jonathan Swift.* vol. 4. Edited by Herbert Davis. Oxford: Basil Blackwell, 1964.

Weidhorn, Manfred. "The Conversation of Common Sense." In *The University Review (Kansas City)* 34 (1967): 3-7.

Wellek, Rene. *A History of Modern Criticism: 1750-1950.* vol 1. New Haven: Yale University Press, 1955.

Wimsatt, William K., Jr., and Cleanth Brooks. *Literary Criticism: A Short History.* New York: Alfred A. Knopf, 1957.

————. *Philosophic Words: A Study of Style and Meaning in the Rambler and Dictionary of Samuel Johnson.* New Haven: Yale University Press, 1948.

LESLIE STEPHEN

Annan, Noel. *Leslie Stephen: The Godless Victorian.* New York: Random House, 1984.

————. "The Intellectual Aristocracy." In *Studies in Social History.* Edited by John H. Plumb. London: Longman's, 1955.

Bicknell, John W. "Leslie Stephen's *English Thought in the Eighteenth Century*: A Tract of the Times." In *Victorian Studies* 6 (1962): 103-20.

Hunt, John. "Mr. Leslie Stephen on English Thought in the Eighteenth Century." In *Contemporary Review* 29 (1877).

Hyman, Virginia. "The Metamorphosis of Leslie Stephen." In *Virginia Woolf Quarterly* 2 (1974): 48-65.

Maitland, F. W. *The Life and Letters of Leslie Stephen.* Bristol: Thoemmes Antiquarian Books Ltd., 1906, reprinted 1991.

VIRGINIA WOOLF

Bell, Barbara Currier, and Carol Ohmann. "Virginia Woolf's Criticism: A Polemical Preface." In *Feminist Literary Criticism: Explorations in Theory.* Edited by Josephine Donovan. Lexington: University Press of Kentucky, 1975.

Bishop, Edward. *Virginia Woolf.* New York: St. Martin's Press, 1991.

Caughie, Pamela L. *Virginia Woolf and Postmodernism.* Chicago: University of Illinois Press, 1991.

Caws, Mary Ann. *Reading Frames in Modern Fiction.* Princeton: Princeton University Press, 1985.

Cuddy-Keane, Melba. "The Politics of Comic Modes in Virginia Woolf's *Between the Acts.*" *PMLA* 105 (March 1990): 273-285.

DeSalvo, Louise. "1897: Virginia Woolf at Fifteen." In *Virginia Woolf: A Feminist Slant.* Edited by Jane Marcus. Lincoln: University of Nebraska Press, 1983.

Dick, Susan. "The Tunnelling Process: Some Aspects of Virginia Woolf's Use of Memory and the Past." In *Virginia Woolf: New Critical Essays.* Edited by Patricia Clements and Isobel Grundy. London: Vision Press Limited, 1983.

Dubino, Jeanne. "A Politics of Exclusion: The Literary Criticism of Virginia Woolf." Doctoral dissertation, University of Massachusetts, 1992.

Eisenberg, Nora. "Virginia Woolf's Last Words on Words: *Between the Acts* and 'Anon'." In *New Feminist Essays on Virginia Woolf.* Edited by Jane Marcus. Lincoln: University of Nebraska Press, 1981.

Freedman, Ralph. *The Lyrical Novel.* Princeton: Princeton University Press, 1963.

Goldman, Mark. *The Reader's Art: Virginia Woolf as Literary Critic.* The Hague: Mouton, 1976.

Graham, John. "Point of View in *The Waves*: Some Services of the Style." *University of Toronto Quarterly* 39, #3 (April 1970): 193-211.

Guiguet, Jean. *Virginia Woolf and Her Works.* Translated by Jean Stewart. London: Hogarth, 1965. Originally published in French as *Virginia Woolf et Son Oeuvre: L'Art et le Quete du Reel.* Paris: M. Didier, 1962.

Hafley, James. *The Glass Roof: Virginia Woolf as Novelist.* Berkeley: University of California Press, 1954.

Herrmann, Anne. *The Dialogic and Difference: "An/Other Woman" in Virginia Woolf and Christa Wolf.* New York: Columbia University Press, 1989.

Hill, Katherine Cicelia. "Virginia Woolf and Leslie Stephen: A Study in Mentoring and Literary Criticism." Doctoral dissertation, Columbia University, 1979.

———. "Virginia Woolf and Leslie Stephen: History and Literary Revolution." *PMLA* 96 (1981): 351-62.

Hussey, Mark. *The Singing of the Real World.* Columbus: Ohio State University Press, 1986.

Hyman, Virginia R. "Late Victorian and Early Modern: Continuities in the Criticism of Leslie Stephen and Virginia Woolf." *English Literature in Transition* 23 (1980): 144-54.

Hynes, Samuel. "Stephen into Woolf." *Sewanee Review* 84 (1976): 510-17.

Johnstone, J. K. *The Bloomsbury Group.* New York: Farrar, Strauss, 1954.

Kronenberger, Louis. "Virginia Woolf as Critic." In *The Republic of Letters: Essays on Various Writers.* New York: Knopf, 1955.

Laurence, Patricia Ondek. *The Reading of Silence: Virginia Woolf and the English Tradition.* Stanford: Stanford University Press, 1991.

Leaska, Mitchell A. *The Novels of Virginia Woolf.* New York: The John Jay Press, 1977.

Lewis, Wyndham. *Men Without Art.* London: Cassell, 1934.

Maika, Patricia. *Virginia Woolf's "Between the Acts" and Jane Harrison's Con/spiracy.* Ann Arbor: UMI Research Press, 1984.

Manuel, M. "Virginia Woolf as the Common Reader." *Literary Criterion* 7.2 (1966): 28-32.

Marcus, Jane. "'No more horses': Virginia Woolf on Art and Propaganda." *Women's Studies* 4 (1977): 265-90.

Marder, Herbert. *Feminism and Art: A Study of Virginia Woolf.* Chicago: University of Chicago Press, 1968.

Meisel, Perry. *The Absent Father: Virginia Woolf and Walter Pater.* New Haven: Yale University Press, 1980.

Minow-Pinkney, Makiko. *Virginia Woolf and the Problem of the Subject.* New Brunswick: Rutgers University Press, 1987.

Moi, Toril. *Sexual/Textual Politics.* London, New York: Methuen, 1985.

Poole, Roger. *The Unknown Virginia Woolf.* New York: Cambridge University Press, 1978.

Ridley, Hilda. "Leslie Stephen's Daughter." *Dalhousie Review* 33 (1953): 65-72.

Rosenbaum, S. P. "An Educated Man's Daughter: Virginia Woolf, Leslie Stephen, and the Bloomsbury Group." In *Virginia Woolf: New Critical Essays.* Edited by P. Clements and I. Grundy. London: Vision; Totowa, N.J.: Barnes and Noble, 1983.

Sharma, Vijay L. *Virginia Woolf as Literary Critic: A Revaluation.* New Delhi: Arnold-Heineman, 1977.

Silver, Brenda. "Virginia Woolf and the Elizabethans." Doctoral dissertation, Harvard University, 1973.

Spivak, Gayatri C. "Unmaking and Making in *To the Lighthouse.*" In *Women and Language in Literature and Society.* Edited by Sally McConnell-Ginet, Ruth Borker, Nelly Furman. New York: Praeger Publishers, 1980.

Steele, Elizabeth. *Virginia Woolf's Sources and Allusions.* New York: Garland Publishing, 1983.

Zwerdling, Alex. *Virginia Woolf and the Real World.* Berkeley: University of California Press, 1986.

THEORETICAL WORKS

Aarsleff, Hans. *From Locke to Saussure.* Minneapolis: University of Minnesota Press, 1982.

Bakhtin, Mikhail. "Discourse in the Novel." In *The Dialogic Imagination.* Edited by Michael Holquist. Translated by Emerson and Holquist. Austin: University of Texas Press, 1981.

―――. *Problems in Dostoevsky's Poetics.* Edited and translated by Caryl Emerson. Minneapolis: University of Minnesota Press, 1984.

―――. "Stylistics of Artistic Discourse: 2. The Construction of Utterances." *Writings of the Circle of Bakhtin.* Translated byWlad Godzich. Minneapolis: University of Minnesota Press, 1984.

Bloom, Harold. *The Anxiety of Influence.* New York: Oxford University Press, 1973.

―――. *A Map of Misreading.* New York: Oxford University Press, 1975.

Edel, Leon. *The Modern Psychological Novel, 1900-1950.* New York: Lippincott, 1955.

Emerson, Caryl. "The Outer Word and Inner Speech: Bakhtin, Vygotsky, and the Internalization of Language." *Critical Inquiry* 10 (1983): 247.

Friedman, Melvin. *Stream of Consciousness.* New Haven: Yale University Press, 1955.

Frye, Northrop. *Anatomy of Criticism.* Princeton: Princeton University Press, 1973.

Humphrey, Robert. *Stream of Consciousness in the Modern Novel.* Berkeley: University of California Press, 1954.

Jakobson, Roman. "Closing statement: linguistics and poetics." *Style in Language.* Edited by Thomas A. Sebeok. Cambridge: M.I.T. Press, 1960.

Lacan, Jaques. "Ego-ideal and ideal ego." *The Seminar of Jaques Lacan: Book I.* Edited by Jaques-Alain Miller. Translated by John Forrester. New York: W. W. Norton & Company, 1988.

Morson, Gary Saul, and Caryl Emerson. *Mikhail Bakhtin: Creation of a Prosaics.* Stanford: Stanford University Press, 1990.

Pater, Walter. "The School of Giorgione." In *Selected Writings of Walter Pater.* Edited with an introduction by Harold Bloom. New York: Columbia University Press, 1974.

Todorov, Tzvetan. *Mikhail Bakhtin: The Dialogical Principle.* Minneapolis: University of Minnesota Press, 1984.

Vygotskii, L. S. *Thought and Language.* Edited and translated by E. Hanfmann and G. Vakar. Cambridge: M.I.T. Press, 1962.

INDEX

.